The Sacrament
of the
Present Moment

The Sacrament
of the
Present Moment

JEAN-PIERRE DE CAUSSADE

Translated by Kitty Muggeridge

HarperSanFrancisco

A Division of HarperCollins*Publishers*

First published in France as *L'Abandon à la Providence divine* by Desclée de Brouwer in 1966. © Desclée de Brouwer 1966.

FIRST HARPERCOLLINS PAPERBACK EDITION PUBLISHED IN 1989.

Designer: Jim Mennick

Library of Congress Cataloging-in-Publication Data

Caussade, Jean-Pierre de, d. 1751.
   THE SACRAMENT OF THE PRESENT MOMENT.

   Translation of: L'Abandon à la providence divine.
   1. Mysticism—Catholic Church.   2. Spiritual life—
Catholic authors.   I. Title.
BV5080.C3 1982   248.4'82   81-48206
ISBN 0-06-061809-4   AACR2
ISBN 0-06-061811-6 (pbk.)

05 RRD H 30 29 28 27 26

Contents

Father de Caussade's Prayer for
the Blessed State of Self-Abandonment

O my God! When will it please thee to grant me the favour of living always in that union of my will with thy heavenly will? Where saying nothing all is said and all is done by leaving all to thee; where we achieve much by surrendering ever more to thy will and yet are relieved of all toil since we place everything in thy care and are concerned only to trust wholly in thee. Blessed state, which, even in the absence of any conscious faith, offers the soul an inward and entirely spiritual disposition. So that, by the habitual inclination of my heart, I may constantly repeat: 'Thy will be done!' Yes, my God, yes to whatever may please thee. May all thy holy wishes be fulfilled. I renounce mine which are blind, perverse and corrupted by that despicable ego, the mortal enemy of thy grace, thy perfect love, thy glory and my sanctification.

Preface

The short mystical treatise which has usually been entitled *Self-Abandonment to Divine Providence* really consists of notes made of talks given by Père Jean-Pierre de Caussade and of extracts from his letters that were carefully preserved by the nuns whose spiritual director he was.

Little is known about the life of this Jesuit priest beyond the bare facts of his career. He lived during the last quarter of the seventeenth century and into the first half of the eighteenth. Although in his day he was by no means unrecognized as a scholar and preacher, there is only one mention of him in the Jesuit calendar, and the only book he published in his life, *Spiritual Instructions on the Various States of Prayer*, appeared anonymously, as by '*un père de la compagnie de Jésus*', and for a time was attributed to a more popular contemporary who used the same *nom de plume*. It was published in 1741 when the quietist heresy was still agitating many Christian minds in France.

It is in the form of a dialogue, with no attempt at fine writing, and its dry style has none of the fiery eloquence that we find in the notes on abandonment. It is a refutation of the quietist heresy and distinguishes true contemplation from its perversion. The key to the errors of quietism is seen in the belief that perfection can be arrived at by giving up all human activity and by complete surrender to the will of God, so that man is no longer interested even in his own salvation. Nothing is required of him—no humility, repentance, self-discipline, worship, thanksgiving, formal prayer, or even pious exercises.

The quietists held that passive meditation or mental prayer, to the exclusion of all else, is the short and easy way to union with God. Père de Caussade emphatically insists that quietism is false mysticism. While his doctrine of self-abandonment may seem to have a certain affinity with what he is refuting, he makes it quite clear in his treatise that we have to strive for our salvation, and that the purely passive attitude of the quietists is ignorant and misguided. 'It is vain for quietism', he declares, 'to reject . . . all tangible means of direction. . . . It is useless to dream of ways to surrender ourselves in which all effort of our own is rejected and total inertia sought'. His doctrine requires an active, not a passive, surrender in body and soul of our will to the will of God. This is the only true contemplation.

The inspiration of Père de Caussade's doctrine is mainly derived from St Francis de Sales, St John of the Cross and the great St Augustine. But two phrases which repeatedly recur throughout his treatise have become especially identified with his name, and embody the whole of his spiritual teaching.

The first, 'Self-abandonment to divine providence' (the title Ramière chose for his version of the treatise) implies a dynamic surrender of ourselves to the will of God. Self-love, self-esteem and pride blind and deafen the soul and can even pollute our good deeds and good will. The self and the ego must be annihilated in order that we may understand what God is telling us and respond to and trust in him alone. The second, and perhaps even more striking phrase, 'The sacrament of the present moment', requires us to do our duty whatever it may be, a carrying out of God's purpose for us, not only this day, or this hour, but this minute, this very minute—now. This is the way we can all strive for spiritual perfection in so far as it is available in this life. Pious saint and humble sinner alike will be given the grace to enable them to do so if they truly long for it.

We must bear in mind that Père de Caussade was advising and encouraging nuns two hundred years ago. Contemplative Marthas and active Marys, some of them aspiring St Teresas of Avila, others lowly handmaidens, all of whom had renounced the world to devote their lives to the service of God. His response, when they wrote telling him of how they suffered and the dire trouble they were having with Lucifer, was a cheerful note saying that he rejoiced over their letter, for their trials and tribulation were a sure sign of God's special love for them!

And yet his doctrine still has a relevant message today for those who find life purposeless in a society abandoned to the fantasies and arrogance of the pursuit of happiness which so quickly becomes a pursuit of pleasure; in which suffering, mental or physical, must be drugged out of existence; in which there is no place for the Cross in Christianity. Those who are ready to believe in God will find comfort and hope in the quest for perfection through surrendering themselves to his will, and discovering in the reality and humiliation of life's trials and tribulation his loving purpose for them.

KITTY MUGGERIDGE

Introduction

I covet for you an experience akin to my first encounter with *The Sacrament of the Present Moment*. I was aboard one of modern technology's finest inventions for solitude—the airplane. Traveling from Santa Barbara, California, to Providence, Rhode Island, I had ample time to read through the entire book slowly, thoughtfully. Since I was released from all interruptions—no telephone to answer, no meetings to attend, no letters to write—I was able to concentrate for the entire day on a single task. Quietly, I was able to ponder each sentence and invite God's Spirit to interpret it into my experience.

The journey from Pacific coast to Atlantic was a long one, but the inward journey that I entered into that day was far greater. It seemed that I was reaching back across the centuries (or was I being reached?) and feeling the pulse of this humble disciple of Christ whose heart throbbed with divine yearnings. I felt caught up into the communion of saints that day and sensed that Jean-Pierre de Caussade had become my teacher in the life of the Spirit. It seemed that de Caussade had joined the cloud of witnesses of Hebrews 12, and was urging me to experience each moment—this very moment—as a holy sacrament. I was encouraged to cease my frantic strivings for holiness and rest in the Light of Christ. It was a hallowed place, a holy day, a sacramental moment.

As wonderful as this experience was, however, I covet for you even more the many little experiences that occurred in the weeks and months that followed. While it is true that none of the events that came later were as radiant as the initial encounter, they were, I believe, even more substantial and lasting in transforming the inner personality. It all started with the persistent questions that began to intrude upon the ordinary events of my day. "In what sense can this experience be a divine sacrament?" "How is Christ mediated to me through this task?" "How can the fulfillment of this present duty be a participation in the life and death of Christ?"

Please understand, I was not dealing with religious tasks such as prayer or holy communion. I could quite readily understand and experience their sacramental character. I was concerned with much more ordinary things, things that made up the bulk of my days — teaching students, answering correspondence, playing with my boys, repairing broken window panes (this happens rather frequently when one's front yard is a miniature soccer field!), paying bills, washing dishes. How could these events take on sacramental significance?

To be sure, this reality was not new to me, for it is a teaching found in the writings of all the devotional masters. And yet, in another sense, it was new or at least broke into my life with new force. Slowly, and without my conscious effort, a greater sense of wonder and spiritual nourishment began to make way into my daily activities. Quiet worship and adoration began to flow out of (rather than in spite of) common tasks. Inward strength and spiritual graces began to slip into my heart as mysteriously as the life of God steals into us through the Eucharist.

I cannot witness that this has been, or is, universally true. More times than I care to remember, tasks have been accomplished without any thought for, or concern about, God's life being mediated to me. Often the present moment is not a sacrament, but a burden to be endured. Other events, such as attempting to discipline the children (complete with angry shouts), still feel decidedly unsacramental. Yet in a strange, almost imperceptible, way even these events are not immune to this heightened awareness of the sacrament of the present moment.

Right in the middle of my preparations for the writing of this introduction, I had to stop to pay the monthly bills. This, I thought to myself, will be the test *par excellence* of experiencing each moment as a divine sacrament. You see, there are two things I utterly detest. One is paying the monthly bills, and the other is being interrupted in the middle of a writing project! Now, I cannot say that I finished the bills in spiritual ecstasy, but I *did* finish them—and, I think, with a measure of grace uncommon to that duty.

All of us—from the youngest to the oldest, from the least able to the most gifted—can enter this journey into the spiritual life to which de Caussade calls us. It takes no special talent, only a yearning to know God and to walk with him. It is a direct and straightforward summons to holiness, this invitation to know the sacrament of the present moment. Perhaps the reading of this little volume, penned by a rather obscure French Jesuit in the eighteenth century, will be the catalyst that will set you on the wonderful lifelong adventure of "self-abandonment to divine providence."

Life

Concerning the life of Jean-Pierre de Caussade, we know none of those things which fire the imagination of modern biographers. We have no idea what he looked like, or how he talked. We do not know his personal quirks, or what hobbies he may have pursued. Although we can pinpoint his date of birth as March 6, 1675, we cannot be certain exactly where he was born, beyond the fact that it was in the province of Quercy in southern France. Perhaps this is just as well, since it forces us to concentrate our energies upon the message that has been given rather than upon the messenger who gave it.

We do have the essential facts of his career, which allow us to place his writings in proper historical context. Indeed, the story of how *The Sacrament* came to be published is a delightful one, as you shall see presently. Much of de Caussade's life was centered in or near the town of Toulouse in southern France, which had a flourishing university and stimulating academic milieu. He grew up in Cahors, just north of Toulouse. When he turned eighteen in 1693, he became a Jesuit novice in Toulouse. Eleven years later he was ordained a priest, and he took his final vows four years after that, in 1708. He taught Greek, Latin, and philosophy in various nearby towns, and then returned to the university at Toulouse for further theological study culminating in a doctorate in theology. In 1720 de Caussade was sent out to preach in many of the towns of southern and central France.

The significant turning point in his career came in the most insignificant of ways—an appointment as spiritual director for the Visitation nuns in the lovely city of Nancy in the northeast corner of France. His appointment was, in the words of the renowned de Caussade authority John Beevers, "a momentous event in the history of spirituality." He came to Nancy in 1729, was called back to Toulouse in 1730, but was able to return to Nancy at the end of 1733, where he remained for nearly six years. While there, de Caussade conducted several conferences on the spiritual life for the nuns and shared with them the simple yet profound reality of his own experience that "God speaks to every individual through what happens to them moment by moment." Cutting through the maze of religious obligations that so often encrust the gospel, he declared, "There remains one single duty. It is to keep one's gaze fixed on the master one has chosen and to be constantly listening so as to understand and hear and immediately obey his will." And again, "the only condition necessary for this state of self-surrender is the present moment in which the soul, light as a feather, fluid as water, innocent as a child, responds to every movement of grace like a floating balloon."

The spiritual inspiration and encouragement of de Caussade's words are attested to by the fact that the original hearers wrote down his messages and then carefully preserved them for over one hundred years before they were ever published. It is the notes of these conferences, along with some of his letters, that comprise the text of *The Sacrament*.

But we must finish de Caussade's story. He left Nancy in 1740 to be the rector of the Jesuit College in Perpignan, and then of the college in Albi. From his letters to the Sisters at Nancy, we see that his tasks there were heavily administrative and that, although he initially found them rather distasteful, he was also able to validate the central principle of his life that obedience to God in the present moment is indeed a holy sacrament. To Sister Marie-Thérèse he wrote:

When I arrived in Perpignan, there was a mass of business—of which I understood nothing—waiting for me to tackle, and a great many people I had to see and try to settle their differences: the Bishop, the Governor, the King's Lieutenant, the Army Staff and members of Parliament. You know how much I detest any formal visits—especially those involving the great figures of the world, yet I found that none of this worried me. I feel such confidence in God that I rise above all these troubles and remain at peace when I should have expected to have been completely overwhelmed by this multitude of complicated affairs.

The final five years of his life were spent once again at the Jesuit house in Toulouse as director of theological students. He died in 1751 at the age of seventy-six.

We today would know nothing of the spiritual genius and remarkable holiness of de Caussade had it not been for the book he never knew he had written. To be sure, he did publish one book anonymously—*Spiritual Instructions in the Form of Dialogues Concerning Different Methods of Prayer*—but it lacks

the fiery eloquence and evangelical enthusiasm so character-
istic of *The Sacrament*, and it would have been totally forgotten
if the notes and letters to the Sisters at Nancy had not been
preserved.

The humble origin of *The Sacrament* is reminiscent of
another book that came to us through an even more obscure
disciple of Christ, Brother Lawrence, who, through his letters
and conversations, gave to the world *The Practice of the Presence of God*. Indeed, the two are of the same spiritual genre
and could almost be considered companion volumes.

Faithfully, the Sisters at Nancy preserved the words of their
spiritual mentor, sharing copies with other convents throughout France. Soon, however, the first rumbles of revolution
were vibrating throughout the land, and the religious houses
were forced underground. Obviously, this was no time for publication; and so for years the cherished writings of de Caussade
were passed clandestinely from hand to hand, much as the
writings of Bonhoeffer were shared with the faithful during
the Nazi terror. Many years later the Sisters, anxious to share
more widely their spiritual treasure, sought counsel about its
publication. Two attempts ended without success, but finally,
in 1861, the learned French Jesuit, Henri Ramière, published
it under the title *L'Abandon à la Providence divine (Self-abandonment to Divine Providence)*. Sadly, though necessarily (in
light of the historical situation), Ramière changed much of de
Caussade's original writings in an attempt to distance them
from anything that smacked of the raging heresy of the day,
quietism. In doing so, however, he blunted de Caussade's
penetrating edge and dampened the fires of his fervent spirit.
Nevertheless, it was quickly recognized as a masterpiece of
Christian spirituality comparable to the writings of St. Francis
de Sales, St. Teresa of Avila, and St. John of the Cross.

Only very recently has there been an attempt to make de
Caussade's writings available in their original vibrancy and

spiritual recklessness. In 1966, Father Olphe-Galliard brought to the French-speaking world a new and definitive edition of de Caussade's letters and lectures. Through them we can once again hear de Caussade's "voice" in all its passion and intensity. And now, through the skillful translation efforts of Kitty Muggeridge (no small accomplishment, given the French style of the early eighteenth century), we have the original arrangement of Father Olphe-Galliard available for the first time to the English-speaking world. Now we too can share in the holiness, the urgency, the sensitivity of this man who lived so long ago, but who speaks so pointedly to contemporary culture.

Relevance

De Caussade's relevance to the modern world is not hard to see. We who find heartfelt abandonment to God distressingly uncomfortable, we who perpetually hack our world into sacred and secular spheres, we who succumb so often to the religion of the "big deal" and ignore the insignificant, we who are constantly boomeranging between works-righteousness and a faith that eschews works, desperately need to hear de Caussade's words of wholeness and integration.

The Sacrament is relevant to our day first because of its refreshing, unchecked yearning for God. Sometimes de Caussade will break unexpectedly into his writing with unashamed doxology. While teaching about the humble context of Christ's birth, he suddenly cries out, "O bread of angels, celestial manna, precious Evangel, sacrament of the present moment, you bring God to the mean surroundings of a lowly stable in a manger among straw and hay." One moment he will be addressing his hearers, and the next moment he is in prayer. While this style is not uncommon in the old writers (one could think of Augustine or even Anselm), de Caussade's oscillation between communication with people and communion with the Father seems so natural as to be almost unconscious.

A favorite concept of de Caussade's is that of utter self-surrender to the divine Center, which incidentally accounts for the original title, *Self-Abandonment to Divine Providence*. He writes, "O boundless submission, it is you that draws God deep into the heart! Let the senses feel what they may, you, Lord, are all my good! Do what you like to this tiny being, let it act, be inspired, be the object of your purpose!" Such extravagant devotion and selfless passion for God is a stern rebuke to the bland Christianity of today. How we need to be prodded out of the ruts of self-centered activity we call living. How we need to see models of reckless, holy zeal for Christ and his Kingdom. De Caussade points the way.

In all of this talk of abandonment and self-surrender, we must not get the idea of harsh rigidity or stringent mortification. Joy, freedom, serenity—these are words much closer to the reality to which de Caussade calls us. In one delightful letter, he speaks of those who insist upon excessive ascetical practices as "extremely unmortified in their mortification."

Nor must we think that he is speaking of a way of life beyond the reach of ordinary disciples. De Caussade writes, "Let us unceasingly impress upon every soul that the invitation of this gentle, loving savior expects nothing difficult or extraordinary of them. He is not making impossible demands on them, he only asks that their good intention be united to his so that he may lead, guide and reward them accordingly. Indeed . . . God is only asking for your heart." Later he writes, "I wish to make all see that everyone can aspire, not to the same specific things, but to the same love, the same surrender, the same God and his work, and thereby effortlessly achieve the most perfect saintliness."

A second reason for *The Sacrament*'s relevance to our day is its utter freedom from all sacred/secular dichotomies. For de Caussade, nothing could be secular—since God's activity permeates all things, even the most trivial. He warns us never to look "for the holiness of things but only the holiness in things." Even time itself is a holy sacrament, for "time is but the history of divine action!"

It is precisely this emphasis upon God's activity in the moments of our personal histories that saves *The Sacrament* from the vaporous, ethereal character of so many of the mystical writers. The spirituality of de Caussade is so utterly practical and down to earth. He takes the moments of our days and the simple duties that make up those moments and gives them sacramental significance. To Sister Marie Thérèse he wrote, "I am sorry that your troubles continue, but I should be much more sorry if you refused to profit by them, at least in the way of making a virtue of necessity." It is obedience to this duty of the present moment that constitutes the path to holiness. This connection with the ordinary events of our lives is what makes de Caussade such a delight to read and sets him apart from so many religious writers.

There is one implication of this practical spirituality that we need to see clearly. All who seek God have a perennial tendency to idolize the means through which he is made known to us. Perhaps it was by means of an altar call that God wonderfully broke into our lives. Perhaps it was in the reciting of a particular liturgy, or the singing of a special hymn, or the reading of a specific book, or in the unmediated quiet of our home, or while we were in a particular posture. We then take that living experience and calcify it and idolize it as *the* way to meet God. Without realizing it, we soon turn a vibrant, life-giving reality into a new legalism, which breathes death.

But de Caussade will have none of such foolishness. For him Christ comes to us in a new and living way each day—indeed, each moment. What was a means of God's grace one moment may become a hindrance the next, since we worship a living Lord, not a static ritual. Hear the daring words of de Caussade: "These blessed results are not produced by any particular circumstance but by what God ordains for the present moment. What was best a moment ago is so no longer because it is removed from the divine will, which has passed on to be changed to form the duty to the next. And it is that duty, whatever it may be, that is now most sanctifying for the soul." We have in these words the invitation to the quickening life of hearing and obeying, rather than the stifling life of rules and regulations. De Caussade continues, "If the divine will ordains that reading is the duty to the present moment, reading achieves that mysterious purpose. If the divine will abandons reading for an act of contemplation, that duty will bring about a change of heart and then reading will be harmful and useless." For those who want life clear-cut and well-defined, such words will feel threatening. But for those who, like myself, have tried the way of law and found it wanting, de Caussade's words sweep over us like a spring breeze inviting us to the adventure.

A third reason this slender volume is singularly appropriate to the contemporary scene is its utter indifference to the spectacular. It is sad to say that much of modern Christianity is captivated by the religion of the "big deal." The slogan of our day is not "might makes right," but "bigger is better." Big churches, big budgets, big names—certainly this is *the* sign of things important. To such idolatry, de Caussade speaks with devastating precision. For him, the focus of God's activity is not center-stage but backstage, in the insignificant moments we often cast aside. "No moment is trivial," observes our mentor, "since each one contains a divine Kingdom, and heavenly sustenance." Listen with the heart to this paean of praise to the insignificant: "Precious moment, how small in the eyes of my head and how great in those of my heart, the means whereby I receive small things from the Father who reigns in heaven! Everything that falls from there is very excellent, everything bears the mark of its maker."

Why this need to focus our attention on these small corners ✓

of life that come to us minute by minute? Because it is there that who we truly are comes to the surface. In the big events—when we are on public display—we can hide what is inside fairly well, and even in the intimacy of our families we can put on a good front for some time; but in the unguarded moment, the true self will surface. And once we can face, before God, who we truly are, we have stepped onto the path of grace that leads to conformity to the image of Christ. But the courage to face the inner monsters takes a faith and trust in God that many of us do not possess (or don't want to possess), and so we busy ourselves with muchness and manyness and undertake our colossal enterprises to avoid looking inside.

One reason de Caussade gives considerable attention to the spiritual values of trials and afflictions is precisely that these, more than all other experiences, bring our true nature to the surface. The high point of this teaching comes in his discussion of "the dark night of faith." These passages are sheer genius in their wisdom and understanding of spiritual formation. De Caussade, of course, is following the lead of St. John of the Cross in his writings on "the dark night of the soul." (Personally, I like de Caussade better for a practical wisdom that I can sink my life into, though St. John is more satisfying as literature.) As you read this "dark night" section, you may be tempted to reject it out of hand, for it is filled with surprising reversals ("Fear itself, suspense, desolation, are verses in the hymns of night") and mystifying paradoxes ("Pessimists are the only optimists, and the two have the same origin"). But we must not be quick to dismiss this experience simply because it is foreign to modern ears, for it is quite common in the devotional masters and is deeply rooted in Scripture.* The desire to sidestep the dark night of faith and enter immediately into the

---

* E.g., Gen. 15 and 22 –Abraham; Gen. 28 – Jacob; Gen. 37 ff.— Joseph; Exod. 2 ff.—Moses; I Kings 19—Elijah; I Sam. 20 ff.—David; Job I ff.— Job; Jer. 20 ff.— Jeremiah; Hab. 1 ff.—Habakkuk; Matt. 4—Jesus; Matt. 26—Peter; Acts 9:16—Paul; and so forth.

bright lights of success and attention is a common malady of contemporary Christian experience.

The fourth point of contemporary relevance of *The Sacrament* is its success in breaking the horns of the age-old dilemma of faith and works, at least that aspect of it that involved holiness of life. (The Reformers dealt with the faith/works issue as it applied to justification; de Caussade dealt with it as it applied to sanctification. In reality the two cannot be neatly separated, but that is another matter altogether and must not muddy the waters of the present discussion.) This is, perhaps, de Caussade's most important contribution to moral theology, and a contribution we would do well to hear. The issue is an ancient one: does heart righteousness come through human effort or the grace of God alone? If the latter, can human effort be done away with? In de Caussade's own day a powerful movement—quietism, led by the Spanish priest, Miguel De Molinos—understood the truth that righteousness comes through God's grace alone. As a result, however, the quietists had abandoned all human activity. They believed that passive meditation or mental prayer was the only way to union with God. Few moderns are tempted by this heresy, but they are often taken in by the opposite notion—namely, that human efforts of worship, prayer, fasting, study, and the like will somehow make us righteous. De Caussade, however, was never tempted by either swing of this pendulum. He understood the central place of God's grace in freeing the heart from all wickedness. Never does he attempt to take the work of the Spirit into human hands. At the same time, he saw clearly the place of human works in placing us before God in such a way that grace may be effectual. This comes out clearly in his call to self-abandonment and obedience to the duty of the present moment. The balance he maintains is superb.

Problems

We would not want to over-idealize the book: there are

weaknesses. Only the naive look for writings that are flawless in all things. The most serious weakness is also the least noticed, because it is not dealt with specifically. It is the tendency to neglect the social dimensions to the spiritual life. What implications would de Caussade's spirituality have for issues of justice and peace? Would it draw us into action on behalf of the poor and oppressed? Would it urge us into a deeper responsibility for our neighbor? Would it intensify our desire to be accountable to the believing community? These are the kinds of questions with which we must struggle if we are to embark upon a spirituality consistent with the way of Christ.

Further, there is a tendency to depreciate reason and analysis in favor of a more inward intuitive grasp of truth. This is unfortunate, since it is quite possible to have both a tough mind and a tender heart. How tragic in our day has been the needless separation between reason and devotion. It is obligatory upon us to affirm a spirituality that loves God with all the mind as well as all the heart and soul (Matt. 22:37).

Finally, there is a tendency to think of miracles, signs, and wonders as needed for the spiritually weak, but unnecessary for the more mature. To be sure, there is an important truth in this. Even Jesus was dismayed at the faith of those who were always looking for a sign (Matt. 11:38). Nevertheless, we need to affirm that manifestations of divine power are the natural outflow of the people of God walking in the Spirit of God and living in the Kingdom of God.

No doubt you noticed that I described all three of these areas as "tendencies." The reason is simple. They do not represent actual errors, only teachings that could be easily misunderstood and distorted. And so, as you can see, I am dealing as much with the problem of our ability to read correctly as I am with de Caussade's ability to write correctly.

Reading with the Heart

Since I have brought up the matter of correct reading, I would like to stay with it for a bit. A word of instruction needs to be given about reading *The Sacrament*, since most moderns have not been trained in the reading of serious books, and a distressing number of Christians have never read even a single substantial work in the spiritual walk. This book makes no attempt to grab you quick and hold you tight. It has no designs to tickle your ears and titillate your fantasies. It promises no easy steps to instant holiness, no guaranteed plan for prosperity and peace of mind.

At first, you may find de Caussade's words hard to understand and his concepts difficult to grasp. That is understandable, because he is speaking of a sacramental way of living with God that most of us glimpse only on the distant horizon. He is leading us into new frontiers of the Spirit, and we have few familiar landmarks by which we can anchor his words. Beyond this, de Caussade wrote two centuries before speed reading, and so he did not know to fill each paragraph with trite cliches and meaningless jargon. As a result, each phrase is pregnant with meaning. If you fail to understand any given sentence, it is best to stay with it for a while—rereading, rethinking, reexperiencing his words until you not only understand their meaning but are gripped by the truth of them.

In his letters, de Caussade himself provides valuable counsel in how to read, counsel that applies equally well to the reading of his own work. "Read quietly, slowly, word for word to enter into the subject more with the heart than the mind. . . . From time to time make short pauses to allow these truths time to flow through all the recesses of the soul and to give occasion for the operation of the Holy Spirit who, during these peaceful pauses and times of silent attention, engraves and imprints these heavenly truths in the heart. . . . Should this peace and rest last for a longer time it will be all the better. When you find that your mind wanders resume your reading and continue thus, frequently renewing these same pauses."

Finally, I would suggest that as you read you not look for a precise logical development of themes. Rather, look for the perceptive insight into human life, look for the winsome combination of wisdom and devotion, look for the sudden burst of joy.

How should we assess *The Sacrament of the Present Moment*? As literature, I think we can say that it is very good. But the real importance and enduring value of this book is not in its ability to stand up to the literary critics. Historically, it is significant because it brings together in a unique blend three streams of Roman Catholic spirituality: Ignatian (St. Ignatius of Loyola, founder of the Jesuit Order), Carmelite (particularly St. John of the Cross and his concept of "The Dark Night of the Soul"), and Salesian (the wise and practical spirituality of St. Francis de Sales, who had such a pronounced influence on C. S. Lewis). But this excites only avid historians; most of us find such matters of only passing interest. No, none of these is sufficient to explain the enduring interest in this slender volume. The greatness of *The Sacrament* and the reason it should be ranked among the classics of Christian devotion is its ability simply and profoundly to lead us to God. De Caussade has read our soul and spoken to our condition. But even more, he has taken us by the hand and led us to the twin paths of trust and obedience that converge onto the highway of godliness.

Perhaps it is most appropriate to conclude this introduction with Jean-Pierre de Caussade at prayer: "How I long to be the missionary of your divine will, O God, to teach the world that there is nothing easier, more ordinary, more available to all than saintliness."

RICHARD J. FOSTER

1. How God Speaks to Us and How We Must Listen to Him

God's Unchanging Word

God still speaks today as he spoke to our forefathers in days gone by, before there were either spiritual directors or methods of direction. The spiritual life was then a matter of immediate communication with God. It had not been reduced to a fine art nor was lofty and detailed guidance to it provided with a wealth of rules, instructions and maxims. These may very well be necessary today. But it was not so in those early days, when people were more direct and unsophisticated. All they knew was that each moment brought its appointed task, faithfully to be accomplished. This was enough for the spiritually-minded of those days. All their attention was focused on the present, minute by minute; like the hand of a clock that marks the minutes of each hour covering the distance along which it has to travel. Constantly prompted by divine impulsion, they found themselves imperceptibly turned towards the next task that God had ready for them at each hour of the day.

Amazing Grace

Such were the hidden motives behind all Mary's behaviour—lowliest and most obedient of creatures. Her reply to the angel, when she was content to say 'Be it unto me according to thy word' (Luke 1:38), summed up the whole mystical teaching of her ancestors. Everything was reduced, as it is now, to the purest and simplest commitment to the will of God in whatever form it might present itself. That exalted and beautiful disposition which was the essence of Mary's soul shines out wonderfully in those simple words. How perfectly it accords with what our saviour wishes us to have unceasingly on our lips and in our hearts—'Thy will be done'. It is true that what was asked of Mary on this momentous occasion was a supreme glory for her, but all that glory would have made no impression on her had not the will of God, which was her only concern, awakened her attention. It was this divine will that ruled her life. Whether her occupations were exalted or lowly, in her eyes they were but shadows, more or less luminous, in which she found it possible both to worship God and to recognize the works of the Almighty. Her spirit, ravished with joy, looked upon everything that she was called upon to do or suffer each moment as the gift of God, who always fills with blessings a heart that is nourished neither by the world nor by fantasy, but by him alone.

The grace of the Most High cast his shadow over Mary. A shadow which was nothing less than the duties, the demands and the suffering of each moment. Which is, in fact, merely a mist similar to that in nature which hangs over tangible objects like a shroud hiding them from our view, and which in the moral and transcendental order, conceals in its obscurity the truth of the Divine Will which alone deserves our attention. And this mist shrouding her faculties, far from deluding Mary, replenished her faith in him who never changes. And so when the Archangel came to her she was ready to receive him. He vanished as he had come and she never saw him again, but the Holy Spirit, accomplishing his earthly mission, entered Mary never to abandon her.

There is little about this amazing happening apparent in the

[2]

Blessed Virgin; at least the gospels make no comment on it. Outwardly Mary's life is represented as simple and ordinary. She does and suffers what others in her situation do and suffer; she visits her cousin Elizabeth as other relations do; she goes to Bethlehem for the census as others do; she lodges in a stable in consequence of her poverty; she returns to Nazareth having been forced to leave on account of Herod's persecution. She lives quietly with Jesus and Joseph who work for their living. Such is the daily bread of the Holy Family. But by what bread do Mary and Joseph nourish their faith? How is what happens moment by moment a sacrament for them? What do they discern beneath the seemingly everyday events which occupy them? What is seen is similar to what happens to the rest of mankind. But what is unseen, that which faith discovers and unravels, is nothing less than God fulfilling his mighty purpose. O bread of angels, celestial manna, precious Evangel, sacrament of the present moment, you bring God to the mean surroundings of a lowly stable in a manger among straw and hay. But to whom do you give yourself? God reveals himself to the humble in small things—'He has filled the hungry with good things' (Luke 1:53)—but the proud, who only attach importance to outward appearances, cannot see him even in big ones.

But what is the secret of how to find this treasure—this minute grain of mustard seed? There is none. It is available to us always, everywhere. Like God, every creature, whether friend or foe, pours it out generously, making it flow through every part of our bodies and souls to the very centre of our being. Divine action cleanses the universe, pervading and flowing over all creatures. Wherever they are it pursues them. It precedes them, accompanies them, follows them. We have only to allow ourselves to be borne along on its tide. Would that it might please God that kings, and their ministers, princes of the Church and of the world, priests, soldiers, commoners, in one word all men, might know how easy it is for them to achieve a sublime holiness! They have only to carry out faithfully the simple duties of a Christian and of their condition, humbly to accept the suffering involved and to submit without question to the demands of Providence in everything that is to be done and suffered. This is that spirituality which sanctified the Patriarchs and the Prophets before the introduction of so many methods of direction and so many masters to teach them. This is the spirituality of all ages and all conditions which surely could not be sanctified more highly or more wonderfully and, at the same time, more easily than by the simple practice of what God, the only director of souls, gives them at each moment to do and suffer, whether it be obedience to the laws of the Church or of princes. If this were so priests would scarcely be required except for the sacraments. For the rest, we could do without them. And those simple souls who are always seeking advice about how to reach God, would be relieved of the heavy and dangerous burdens needlessly imposed on them by those who take pleasure in exercising control over them.

2. How to Arrive at the State of Self-Surrender and How to Act Before Reaching It

God Living in Souls and Souls Living in God

There is a time when the soul lives in God and there is also a time when God lives in the soul. What is appropriate to one of these conditions is inappropriate to the other. When God lives in souls, they must surrender themselves totally to him. Whereas when souls live in God, they must explore carefully and scrupulously every means they can find which may lead them to their union with him. All their paths are clearly marked—their reading, values and ideas. Their Guide is by their side, and when the time comes for them to speak for themselves all is clear. But when God lives in souls there is nothing of themselves left, save what comes from his inspiration. For them there are no plans, no longer any clearly marked paths. They are like a child whom one leads wherever one wills and who sees only what is pointed out to him. No more recommended reading for these souls. Frequently they are deprived of any spiritual direction. God leaves them with no other support than himself. They dwell in darkness, oblivion, rejection; suffer distress and misery without knowing from where or whence help will come. Calm and untroubled, they must wait for succour, their eyes turned towards heaven. And God, who seeks no purer aspirations in his loved ones than the total surrender of their whole selves, in order that they may exist by grace and divine action alone, himself replaces the books, ideas, self-assurance, advice and wise guidance of which they are deprived. Everything that others painstakingly discover is revealed to these souls in their solitude. And what others carefully store up until such time as they choose to use it, they receive and relinquish according to their needs, keeping only what God is willing to give them in order that they may live through him alone. Others undertake an infinite number of tasks to glorify God. These simple souls often find themselves discarded in some forgotten corner, like pieces of broken crockery for which no further use can be found. Here, neglected by men, but in possession of God through their pure, steadfast and passionate, though deeply tranquil, love, they make no effort of their own. They know only that they must allow themselves to be carried along in God's hands, to serve him in his own way. Often they will not know for what purpose, but God knows it well. The world will think them useless. Indeed, appearances favour this judgement, though the truth is that secretly and through unknown channels these souls pour out infinite blessings on people who may never have heard of them, of whose existence they are themselves unaware.

Waiting on God

Everything in these solitary souls speaks to us of God. God gives their silence, quiet, oblivion and isolation, their speech and their actions a certain virtue, which, unknown to themselves, affects others. And, just as they themselves are guided by the chance actions of innumerable creatures that are unwittingly influenced by the grace of God, they, too, guide and sustain many souls with whom they have no connection and no commitment to do so. It is God acting in unexpected and often mysterious ways. So that they are like Jesus, from whom escaped an unseen virtue with power to heal others. But with this difference that, more often than not, they are unconscious of any virtue escaping from them or even that they have co-operated in any way. It is like some mysterious balm whose unaccountable blessing is unconsciously felt.

The condition of these simple souls, then, can be compared to that of Jesus and the Blessed Virgin and St Joseph. It is a question of waiting on the good pleasure of God. That is to say, to be and to function in a continuing state of passivity inspired only by his loving kindness. But it is important to distinguish his mysterious, unpredictable, unaccountable and undefined will—his will of pure providence—from his specific and pre-determined will which, however, no one must ignore. Leaving aside this specific will, those with whom we are concerned are by definition dependent on that other will, the will of pure providence. And this is why their lives, though very extraordinary, appear commonplace and quite ordinary. They fulfil their religious and other duties, as others apparently do likewise. Examine them for the rest and you will discover nothing striking or special about them. They are not in any way unusual. What might distinguish them cannot be detected through the senses. It is that continual dependence on the Supreme Will in which they exist, and which seems to take care of everything for them. It gives them mastery over themselves through the habitual surrender of their hearts and, whether they obey it consciously or unconsciously, directs them to the service of others.

There are no honours or rewards for work seemingly so unimportant and unprofitable as far as the world is concerned. These souls, who by their very nature are disengaged from nearly all earthly endeavour, are poorly equipped for the world of commerce or business, or the concerns and conduct of industry. They are no use in a worldly sense. Only the feebleness of their intellect, their low spirits and their lack of resolve are apparent. They seem to be hopeless, dull-witted, improvident and faint-hearted. There is no sign in them of what education, study and reflection give to men. They appear to be simpletons. All that is visible is what nature gives to children before they have passed through the hands of teachers responsible for their training. Their smallest faults are noted and, though not more serious, offend more than they do in children. God takes everything from them except their innocence, in order that they may possess him alone. The world, not understanding this mystery, judges these souls on appearances and can find nothing to esteem or even tolerate in them. It rejects and despises and ridicules them. The closer they are seen, the less can be made of them and the more they are criticized. No one knows what to think or say about them. And yet, nevertheless, there is something indefinable that speaks in their favour. Instead of listening, however, or at least suspending judgement, the world chooses to be malicious, to spy on their actions and to judge them according to worldly standards. And just as the pharisees could never tolerate the ways of Jesus, so the world looks upon them with so much prejudice that everything they do is considered either reprehensible or ridiculous.

Alas, these poor souls think no better of themselves. United as they are to God through faith and love alone, they are bewildered and confused. And, when they compare themselves with others who are regarded as saints and who are able to observe all sorts of regulations, who merely follow a set of rules, they are covered with confusion.

Their humiliation is what gives them an air of melancholy and draws from them those deep sighs. We must remember that Jesus was at once God and Man. As Man he was humiliated, but as God he was glorified. These souls know only humiliation and have no share in his glory, which accounts for their dismay. In the eyes of the world they are as Jesus was in the eyes of Herod and his court.

Belonging Wholly to God

It is easy to conclude from all this that these committed souls are unable to take any interest in ambition, fashions or other worldly matters, or in high society, important projects, or refinements of speech or behaviour. This would assume that they are in control of their own lives, which in itself would preclude the state of surrender in which they find themselves. A state in which one discovers how to belong wholly to God through the complete and total assignment of all rights over oneself—over one's speech, actions, thoughts and bearing; the employment of one's time and everything relating to it. There remains one single duty. It is to keep one's gaze fixed on the master one has chosen and to be constantly listening so as to understand and hear and immediately obey his will. Nothing so well illustrates this condition as that of a servant whose sole duty lies in obeying instantly whatever orders his master may give him, and not employing his time on his own affairs, which he must put aside in order to be to his master all things at all times.

The Path of Pure Duty

So these souls are by their nature solitary, free and detached from everything, in order that they may contentedly love the God who possesses them in peace and quiet, and faithfully fulfil their duty to the present moment according to his wishes. They do not allow themselves to question, turn back, or consider the consequences, the causes or the reasons. It must suffice them simply to follow the path of pure duty as though there was nothing in the world but God and this pressing obligation. Thus, the present moment is like a desert in which simple souls see and rejoice only in God, being solely concerned to do what he asks of them. All the rest is left behind, forgotten and surrendered to him. God uses these souls to undertake and carry out his secret purpose, whether it occupies them passively within themselves or actively outside themselves. Their participation in this outward employment is voluntary and tangible yet at the same time innate and mystical. That is to say that God, satisfied that in their willingness he has found all he needs to accomplish whatever he may ordain, spares them trouble by bringing to pass for them what otherwise they would have had to achieve through their own endeavour. It is as though someone seeing a friend wishing to make a journey, were to do him a good turn by forthwith entering into him and going on the journey on his behalf; so that the friend wishing to make the journey has, at the same time, made it by virtue of this mysterious substitution. The journey will have been free, being the result of a free decision on the part of him at whose expense it was made. It will be transcendental because it will have been accomplished without effort on the part of the friend. Finally, it will be mystical because its origin is unseen.

The Discipline of Passive Surrender

But to return to the kind of participation illustrated by this imaginary journey which, it will be noticed, is totally different from the way we submit to defined obligations, which is neither mystical nor inspired but rational and intentional. For obedience to God's undefined will depends entirely on our passive surrender to it. We put nothing of ourselves into it apart from a general willingness that is prepared to do anything or nothing, like a tool that, though it has no power in itself, when in the hands of the craftsman, can be used by him for any purpose within the range of its capacity and design. Whereas our obedience to the declared and defined will of God consists in the normal course of vigilance, care, attention, prudence and discretion according to how far we are helped by grace in our customary endeavours. And so we leave God to act in everything, reserving for ourselves only love and obedience to the present moment. For this is our eternal duty. This compelling love, steeped in silence, is required of every soul. They must foster it unceasingly and always be prepared to meet any demands it may make, even though this means taking action. This obedience to the present moment is, moreover, an act whereby they dedicate themselves totally to the external will of God as a matter of course. This is their rule, method, law and way. Pure, simple and sure, it is a straight path along which souls walk with courage and faith, looking neither to the right nor to the left, unconcerned with everything else. Everything over and above this, they receive passively and respond to submissively. In short, they are active in everything needed for the fulfilment of their duty to the present moment, but passive and submissive and self-forgetting in everything else; only meekly waiting on the divine will. Nothing is more secure than this straightforward way, as there is nothing clearer, easier, sweeter or less subject to error and illusion. One loves God, does one's Christian duty, frequents the sacraments, observes the external religious practices that are required of everyone. One obeys superiors, civil duties are performed, impulses of the flesh, the blood and the devil are continually resisted. For no one is more scrupulous in acquitting themselves of all these obligations than those set on this course. This being so, how is it then that they are so often exposed to criticism? Often, having acquitted themselves like other Christians of the requirements of the strictest theologians, they are expected to perform prodigious acts of piety which even the Church herself does not insist upon. And, should they not be forthcoming, they are accused of deluding themselves.

Is a Christian who goes about his human and other temporal affairs considered in error because he confines himself to keeping the commandments of God and the Church without either meditation, contemplation, study of the scriptures or submitting to special spiritual discipline? No one dreams of accusing or even suspecting him of anything of the sort. Let us be consistent then. If such a Christian as this is left in peace, it is only fair not to trouble those who not only fulfil the minimum requirements at least as well as he does, but in addition include inward and outward practices in piety of which he is not even aware or, if he is, to which he is indifferent.

This prejudice goes so far as to insist, in spite of everything, that these souls are at fault because, after having submitted to everything the Church ordains, they consider themselves ready and free to devote themselves unhindered to God's secret purpose for them and to follow the guidance of his grace after having fulfilled their specific obligations. In short, they are condemned because the time others give to amusements and temporal matters, they devote to loving their God. This is certainly unjust. So long as a person abides by generally accepted standards, so long as he makes his confession once a year, no one questions or bothers him, being content merely to urge him now and again (but not too persistently) to aspire to something a little higher but without pressing him too hard. Should he, however, be changed and raise his standard of spiritual behaviour above the normal level he is at once overwhelmed with dogmas, rules and rituals; and if he does not bind and pledge himself to the observance of established practices of piety, if he does not constantly carry them out, what happens? The worst is feared for him and his way becomes questionable. Don't we realize that those practices, good and holy though we suppose them, are but the way that leads to the divine union? Why, then, insist that he must stay on the road when he has actually reached his goal?

The Stirrings of Grace

This is, however, what is required of souls suspected of deluding themselves. They have made the journey, like the others, from the beginning. They are like them, familiar with the way and have followed it faithfully. It would be useless at this stage to insist that they should retrace their steps. Since God, touched by their efforts to go forward in this way, goes ahead of them, as it were, to accomplish his purpose of leading them to this happy union with him; since they have reached that beautiful region where one breathes only submission and where one begins to possess God with love; since, at last, God himself, in his loving kindness, has taken the place of all their troubles and cares, and has made himself the mainspring of their actions, these practices have lost their virtue for them. They are nothing more than the path which they have already trodden and long since left behind. Therefore, to insist that they should resume them, or continue to observe them, is to try to force souls to renounce the goal they have already reached, in order to take again the path which led them to it.

This would be a waste of time and trouble. Experienced souls in whom God lives will be deaf to exhortations to retrace their steps. Untouched by the noise and the tumult, they will remain quite undisturbed in that secret peace so favourable to the expression of their love. This is where they will come to rest. In other words, this is the straight path traced by God himself, on which they will always walk with him. They will continue along it; all their duties to the present moment are marked along its course, one by one they will fulfil them unconfused, unhurried. For the rest, they will keep themselves entirely free, waiting always to obey the stirrings of grace as soon as they make themselves felt, and to surrender themselves to the care of Providence.

These souls are in that state which can only be arrived at with the help of an exceptional adviser. If this is not available they wait patiently and wisely, knowing God will never leave them without help, until they chance to cross the path of someone in whom they instinctively confide, without knowing who he may be or whence he comes. They are inspired by God. It is his way of letting his light shine, even if only momentarily. This is how he always provides us with spiritual guidance until, after we have walked with him in complete surrender, he removes us from this world.

3. The Virtue and Practice of Surrendering Ourselves

Confined to the Present Moment

It is necessary to be disengaged from all we feel and do in order to walk with God in the duty of the present moment. All other avenues are closed. We must confine ourselves to the present moment without taking thought for the one before or the one to come. For is not God's law always under cover, as it were? Something will prompt us to say: 'At the moment I have a liking for this person or this book, or an inclination to take or offer this advice, to make such a complaint, to confide in or listen to this person, or to give away this or to make that.' These stirrings of grace must be followed without relying for a single moment on our own judgement, reason or effort. It is God who must decide what we shall do and when, and not ourselves. When we walk with God, his will directs us and must replace every other guidance.

Each moment imposes a virtuous obligation on us which committed souls faithfully obey. For God inspires them with a desire to learn one moment what, in the next, will uphold them in the practice of virtue. They are drawn to read this or that, to observe and reflect upon the smallest happening. In this way everything that they learn and hear is fresh in their mind and no dedicated novice will carry out her duty better than they do.

In all that these souls do, they are aware only of an urge to act without knowing why. All they can say is: 'I have an urge to write, read, question or observe this. I obey this urge and God, who inspires it, supplies me with a store of knowledge which subsequently I am able to use to the advantage of myself and others.' This is why they must always remain simple, pliant and responsive to the slightest prompting from these almost imperceptible impulses. God, who possesses them, may make use of them in any way for his glory. If they were to resist these impulses, like those who depend on their own efforts and initiative, they would be depriving themselves of countless things essential for the fulfilment of future obligations to the present moment. Since people do not recognize this, such souls are criticized and blamed for their simplicity and they, who blame no one, who are tolerant and understanding of all sorts and conditions, find themselves despised by the falsely wise, who are unable to savour that sweet and refreshing submission to God's commands.

Could the worldly wise tolerate that incessant wandering of the Apostles who never settled anywhere? Likewise the pious in general cannot tolerate those who thus wait on divine guidance for their moment to act. Only a very few do, and God, who teaches men through their fellows, always puts them in touch with those who are faithful in their submission to him.

God Revealed in the Present Moment

When God wishes to be the whole life of souls, and in a mysterious and secret way, to be himself their perfection, all individual ideas, understanding, endeavours, searching, or argument become a source of fantasy. And when, after several experiences of the folly of their own efforts, they finally recognize their futility, they discover that God has blocked every other avenue in order that they should walk with him alone. Then, convinced of their nothingness, and that everything deriving from themselves is damaging, they surrender themselves to God so as to have nothing but him, from him and through him. And so God becomes the source of life for these souls, not through ideas or enlightenment or reasoning—all that is but a fantasy to them now—but hidden in the operation and truth of his grace. The working of this divine process being unknown to them, souls receive its blessing, its substance and its truth in all sorts of events which they imagine to be their ruin. There is no remedy for this darkness but to sink into it. God reveals himself in all things through faith. We are nothing more than blind creatures, invalids as it were, who, ignorant of the virtue of medicines, resent their bitter taste, often imagining they are poison. And all the crises and weakness seem to justify our fears. Nevertheless, in spite of this mortal threat, obeying the doctor's orders, we swallow the medicines he prescribes and recover.

Before, souls could see wherein lay the perfection of their faith by the light of reason. But now in their present state, it is no longer so. Now they discover that perfection comes to them, not through reason, enlightenment or reflection, but through every affliction sent by God, through their duty to the present moment, and through impulses with nothing good about them, though not actually sinful, and which seem utterly remote from the sublime wonder and glory of virtue.

It is in these afflictions, which succeed one another each moment, that God, veiled and obscured, reveals himself, mysteriously bestowing his grace in a manner quite unrecognized by souls who feel only weakness in bearing their cross, distaste for performing their duty, and capable only of the most mediocre spiritual practices. All saintly ideals are but an inward reproach to their wretched, despicable nature. Everything written about the lives of the saints condemns them. These souls are unable to justify themselves. They see saintliness in a light which makes them despair because they no longer have the strength to achieve it. They do not think of their faint-heartedness as divinely ordained, but as cowardice. All their friends and those who are admired for the brilliance of their virtues or the loftiness of their aspirations, look upon them with contempt. 'What a saint!' they sneer. And souls, believing them, dismayed by all the useless efforts they have made to rise above their failings, are overcome with shame and have nothing to say for themselves.

God Is Everywhere

Nevertheless, a preoccupation with God tells them unconsciously that all will be well provided they leave him to do what he will, and live by faith alone—like Jacob who said: 'Surely the Lord is in this place and I knew it not' (Genesis 28:16). You are seeking God, dear sister, and he is everywhere. Everything proclaims him to you, everything reveals him to you, everything brings him to you. He is by your side, over you, around and in you. Here is his dwelling and yet you still seek him. Ah! You are searching for God, the idea of God in his essential being. You seek perfection and it lies in everything that happens to you—your suffering, your actions, your impulses are the mysteries under which God reveals himself to you. But he will never disclose himself in the shape of that exalted image to which you so vainly cling.

Although Martha sought to please Jesus by waiting on him, Mary was content to sit at his feet. And yet he misled even her, for, while she was looking for him as she knew him, he appeared to her as a gardener. And when the Apostles saw Jesus they took him for a ghost. So God hides himself in order to raise souls up to that perfect faith which will discover him under every kind of disguise. For once they knew God's secret, disguise is useless. They say: 'See him! There he is, behind the wall, looking through the trellis, in at the window!' O Divine Love, conceal yourself, leap over our suffering, make us obedient!

Mystify us, arouse and confuse us. Shatter all our illusions and plans so that we lose our way, and see neither path nor light until we have found you, where you are to be found and in your true form—in the peace of solitude, in prayer, in submission, in suffering, in succour given to another, and in flight from idle talk and worldly affairs. And, having tried all the known ways and means of pleasing you and not finding you any longer in any of them, we remain at a loss until, finally, the futility of all our efforts leads us at last to leave all to find you henceforth, you, yourself, everywhere and in all things without discrimination or reflection. For, how foolish it is, O Divine Love, not to see you in all that is good and in all creatures. Why, then, try to find you in what you are not? O Divine Love, how is it that you are being sought in other symbols than those you have chosen for your sacraments; whose very mystery, surely, is a witness to the need for obedience and faith?

4. Surrendering to God:
The Wonders It Performs

A Divine Chain of Events

What profound truths lie hidden in this condition! How true that all suffering, every action, all the allurement of God's word, reveals him in a way which can only be described as the greatest of all mysteries! How true, therefore, that the holiest of lives is mysterious in its simplicity and humility. O, glorious celebration! Eternal bounty! God forever available, forever being received. Not in pomp or glory or radiance, but in infirmity, in foolishness, in nothingness. God chooses what human nature discards and human prudence neglects, out of which he works his wonders and reveals himself to all souls who believe that is where they will find him.

Thus wide horizons, sure ground and solid rock can only be found in that vast expanse of the divine will which is eternally present in the shadows of the most ordinary toil and suffering; and it is in these shadows that God hides the hand which up-holds and supports us. This is all souls need to know in order to achieve that sublime surrendering of themselves which will free them from contentious argument and the need to account for their actions; they will not know why they do them for they are not based on reason but inspired by an unseen power which cannot be explained. But, since it is God's work, if allowed to take its course, it will justify the consequences. 'Day unto day

uttereth speech and night unto night showeth knowledge'
(Psalm 18:3, Vulgate). Words are no longer necessary to
explain what is not based on reason, for they can only express
our ideas and where there are no ideas of what use are they? To
give a reason for our action? But we do not know that reason
since its origin is unknown. We must therefore allow each
moment to be the cause of the next; the reason for what precedes being revealed in what follows, so that everything is
linked firmly and solidly together in a divine chain of events.
The world of ideas, imagination, argument no longer nourishes
and sustains souls. They no longer see or know where they are
going, no longer depend on an effort of will to overcome the
fatigue or endure the hardship of the journey. Everything happens in a profound sense of their own helplessness. The way
opens up before them as they walk and they follow it with unfaltering step. Pure, holy, innocent and true they walk in the
straight path of God's commandments, discovering along the
way a perfect trust in God himself. Souls no longer try to reach
him through reading, endless speculation or inner supplications.
Books and disputation are irrelevant, for God seeks them out
and reveals himself to them. No need now to look for the way
that leads to him, for he himself has prepared it. It lies before
them well beaten and clearly marked. All that remains is to be
ready to grasp God who is close beside them at each step and
each moment in all the various situations that arise in never
ending succession along their way.

And so we have only to welcome divine eternity in the
passing shadows of time. Shadows that change, though the
eternity they hide is changeless. Completely detached from all
else, we must fling ourselves headlong unto the bosom of
divine providence, constantly pursuing love by way of affliction, duty and disinterested hopes and desires.

How clear and shining this way is! I proclaim it openly so
that everyone may know that sanctification consists of enduring

[21]

moment by moment all the trials and tribulation it brings, as though they were clouds behind which God lay concealed.

The only condition necessary for this state of self-surrender is the present moment in which the soul, light as a feather, fluid as water, innocent as a child, responds to every movement of grace like a floating balloon. Such souls are like molten metal filling whatever vessel God chooses to pour them into.

It is important to remember that in this state, this way of faith, everything that takes place in body and soul and all earthly phenomena has a ghostly appearance. This is not surprising; it is its nature, for God carries out his purposes triumphantly in those dark shadows; in failures, in bodily sickness, and spiritual weakness. But everything succeeds and turns out for the best in his hands, and it is through what most distresses human beings that he contrives and accomplishes his highest designs. We know indeed that 'all things work together for good to them that love God.'

The Instinct of Faith

He directs our lives from these shadows so that, when the senses are scared, faith, taking everything in good part and for the best, is full of courage and confidence.

Since we know that divine action understands, directs and creates everything apart from sin, we must love and worship all it does, welcoming it with open arms. In joy and confidence we must override everything in order to bring about the triumph of faith. That is the way to honour and acknowledge God.

To live by faith, then, is to live in joy, confidence, certainty and trust in all there is to do and suffer each moment as ordained by God. However mysterious it may seem, it is in order to awaken and maintain this living faith that God drags the soul through tumultuous floods of so much suffering, trouble, perplexity, weariness and ruin. For faith is needed to discover in all this God and that divine life which can neither

[22]

be seen nor felt but, nevertheless, in some mysterious way, unmistakably reveals itself. Death in the body, damnation in the soul, ruin in the world are the nourishment and support of faith, which, breaking through these, holds on to the hand of God offering life wherever there is no sign of sin. Faithful souls, full of confidence, must see God in everything, hidden in a cloud, whose closer presence disturbs and scares the senses.

Nothing is more noble than a faithful heart that sees only life divine in the most grievous toil and peril. Even when required to swallow poison, walk the plank, be the slave of a tyrant, finding it in abundance, not just drop by drop, but in a torrent, flooding and engulfing the soul. An army of such soldiers would be invincible. For the instinct of faith is an uplifting of the heart and a reaching over and above everything that happens.

Living by faith and the instinct of faith are the same thing. It is joy in God's goodness and trust founded on the hope of his protection; a faith which delights in and accepts everything with good grace. It is an indifference and a readiness to face any situation or condition or person. Faith is never sad, sick or in mortal sin. Faith always lives in God and his works even when they seem harmful and blind the senses. Scared, they suddenly cry out: 'Wretch, you're lost! At the end of your tether!' And faith immediately replies yet louder: 'Hold fast, march on, fear nothing.'

Led Past Perils and Monsters

Except in the case of a specific illness which, by its nature, requires lying in bed and appropriate treatment, all our languors and feebleness are mere illusions and fantasies which we must face courageously and with confidence. These are allowed or sent by God in order to exercise our faith and submission which is the true cure. We must bravely pursue our way through the tribulations and suffering ordained by God, recklessly using our bodies as hired hacks to be mercilessly worked to death. That is worth more than a lifetime of ease which weakens our strength of mind. This strength of mind has untold power to uphold a frail body, and one year of courageous endeavour, always trying to maintain the bearing of a child of grace and good will, is worth a century of timid caution. Ah! what is there to fear in following divine guidance? Led, upheld, protected, we need only to put a brave face on things. The terrifying objects put in our way are nothing. They are only summoned in order to embellish our lives with glorious adventures. It involves us in all kinds of difficulties in which human ingenuity, unable to discover or imagine a way out, realizes its own feebleness and finds itself at a loss and confounded. It is then that God's purpose is manifest in all its radiance, rescuing souls more miraculously than any writer of fantastic tales, who, straining every effort of his imagination in the seclusion of his study, unravels the intrigues and perils of his imaginary heroes and always brings their adventures to a happy conclusion. It leads souls far more ingeniously past mortal perils, past monsters, hell-fire, demons and their snares and carries them up to heaven. All are the subject of mystical tales far more beautiful and amazing than any invented by the crude imagination of mortal men.

Come then, past the perils and monsters, guided and upheld by that sure unseen hand which is the invincible, infallible hand of God. March on fearlessly to the end in peace and joy, turning everything we meet with into victory. It is to fight and to conquer that we are marching. As many steps as we take under such a banner, my sisters, so many triumphs! The Holy Spirit of God, pen in hand, the book open before him, continues the sacred story which has yet to be told. Its theme will not be exhausted until the end of time. It is none other than the record of God's guidance and his purposes for man. It remains for us to take part in that story and to supply the sequel by obeying his commands in all we do and suffer. No, no! all that is not given us for our ruin, but in order that we may supply the plot of the holy scripture which unfolds every day. The Love of God, submission to his divine action; that is what is necessary to sanctify souls, that is all that is required of them; and their faithfulness in responding to it is what gives them grace. Sanctified souls are only souls wholly committed to the divine will by the help of grace. Everything beyond this is the work of God and not of man, who must accept it in blind surrender and complete indifference. This is the only condition God asks of him. The rest he selects and decides according to his designs, as a builder selects and allocates his bricks.

Cherishing God and His Divine Order

And so God and his divine order must be cherished in all things, just as it is, without asking for anything more; whatever he may offer us is not our business but God's, and what he ordains is best. How simple is this perfect and total surrender of self to the word of God! And there, in continual self-forgetfulness to be forever occupied in loving and obeying him, untroubled by all those doubts and perplexities, reverses and anxieties which attend the hope of his salvation and true perfection! Come, my sisters, forward, head held high above everything in and around us, always rejoicing in God, rejoicing in all that he does and makes us do. Beware of imprudently engaging in any of those disquieting speculations which waylay the spirit, leading it needlessly astray. Let us cross this labyrinth by leaping over it, not by following false trails which lead nowhere.

Over the languors, sickness, faint-heartedness, dryness, ill-humour, snares of the devil and of men, their suspicion, jealousy, disastrous ideas and prejudices, my soul, let us go. Let us fly like an eagle above all those dark clouds with eyes ever fixed on the sun and on our duty which is its rays. And although it is not in our power ever to forget them, we must always remember that our life is not only one of the senses. Let us live in that sublime region where God and his will govern an eternity which remains unvarying, changeless. For in this entirely spiritual existence the transcendental, the inexpressible, keep souls infinitely remote from everything connected with earthly shadows and tangible creation and all the anxiety and agitation and constant change of mood experienced by the senses, where everything happens inconsequentially and in a perpetual state of flux. God and his purpose is the eternal object and enchantment of the faithful heart, and in its blessedness brings true happiness. In this blissful state the heart influences all earthly creation which, at present, is merely a prey to monsters, ill omens and savage attacks, and through them, terrifying though they are, will make it shine like the sun. For body and soul here below are fashioned of gold, iron, stone and linen and, like these diverse substances, do not reveal their brilliance and purity until they have been reshaped, melted down, broken up, and shrunk. Everything that has to be endured here below at the hand of God the divine workman, who is love, only draws them to him. The faithful, knowing God's secret, remain in perfect peace and all that happens, instead of terrifying, reassures them. They accept everything as a blessing and live in forgetfulness of what God is doing in order to devote themselves entirely to their task of unceasing love that inspires them faithfully and exactly to fulfil their obligations.

Everything in those who have surrendered themselves is shaped by divine action, excepting their sins which are slight and can even be turned to good account by it. I mean all those impressions made on them by the tasks, whether distressing or consoling, which the divine will constantly imposes on them for their own good. For these are the impressions which affect them most deeply throughout their lives and influence them more profoundly than any others they experience. To discover God in them is the object of faith; to follow and surrender to him is its exercise.

5. Perfect Faith

The Trinity of Excellent Virtues

Perfect faith is faith, hope and charity embodied in a single act uniting the heart to God and his purpose, becoming one single virtue, one uplifting of the heart to him in complete surrender. How otherwise can this divine unity, this spiritual essence, be expressed? How can its nature and meaning be truly conveyed? How the concept of three in one illumined? It is simply the fulfilment and enjoyment of God and his purpose. We see the beloved object, we worship him, we hope all things from him. We may call this perfect love, perfect hope, perfect faith: that trinity of mystical and theological virtues known simply as perfect faith. In this state of perfect faith nothing is more certain as far as God is concerned, and for the heart, nothing more uncertain. And in the union of the two, certainty of faith comes from God and from the doubting heart faith tempered by uncertainty and hope.

O how desirable is the trinity of these excellent virtues! You must believe, then, my sisters, hope, love with the Holy Spirit, God's gift, in your hearts, suffusing your whole being. Therein lies the comfort of the divine presence. That is the promise, the mystical revelation, the pledge of the happy outcome of our future destiny.

In souls set on fire this feeling is perfect love, because of the voluptuous torrent which floods all the faculties with an abundance of confidence and light. But in souls intoxicated by the Holy Spirit, when obscurity and darkness are total, it is perfect faith. For perfect love sees, feels and believes, whereas perfect faith believes without seeing or feeling. That is the difference between them and it is only one of degree, since, as in fact perfect faith does not lack love, so perfect love lacks neither surrender nor faith. It depends which of the two dominates and the differing proportion of these two virtues in that touch of the Holy Spirit makes the diversity of all transcendental states. As God is able to blend them in an infinite number of ways, every soul receives this precious touch in a unique and special way which nevertheless always remains faith, hope and charity. Surrender of self is the universal means whereby we may receive virtue from this touch of the Holy Spirit in one form or another. All souls cannot hope to be the same or to reach the same state under these divine influences, but they can all be united with God, all surrender themselves to his action, be wedded to his purposes, receive their own unique touch of the Holy Spirit; and in the end all be participators in his majesty and privileges. It is a kingdom in which every soul can aspire to a crown, whether one of love or of faith; it will always remain a crown, always the kingdom of God. It is true that some may be in darkness and some in light, but what does it matter, providing all are united in God and his action? For what are they seeking? Fame? Distinction? Perfection? No. They are seeking God himself and how they find him is a matter of indifference.

Surrendering to Divine Action

Let us not preach perfect faith or perfect love, suffering or blessings to all. These are not given to all, nor yet in the same way. But to every pure heart fearing God, let us talk of surrendering to divine action and make it clear to all that they will receive by this means that special state which has been chosen and ordained for them for all eternity. Let us not discourage, impede or separate anyone from that height of perfection to which Jesus calls us; for he demands that all should submit to the will of his father and become part of his mystical body whose members can only truly call him master when their will is totally in accord with his. Let us unceasingly impress upon every soul that the invitation of this gentle, loving saviour expects nothing difficult or extraordinary of them. He is not making impossible demands on them, he only asks that their good intention be united to his so that he may lead, guide and reward them accordingly.

Indeed, dear sisters, God is only asking for your hearts. If you truly seek this treasure, this kingdom where God alone reigns, you will find it. Your heart, if it is totally surrendered to God, is itself that treasure, that very kingdom you long for and are seeking. When we long for God and his will we rejoice in it and that rejoicing is the fulfilment of our longing. To love God is to long earnestly to do so. Loving, we wish to be the instrument of his action so that his love can operate in and through us. Divine action responds to the willingness and good intentions of the pure and simple, not to their intelligence, nor to any precautions they may take, plans they may form, thoughts they may have or means they may adopt on their own initiative. All these can lead them astray—they often do. But their honesty and good intentions never betray them. Provided God sees that their intentions are good he ignores the rest and accepts as done that which they would infallibly have done had they been strengthened by a clearer insight.

Those with good intentions, therefore, have nothing to fear. They can only fall under that almighty hand which guides and supports them in all their shortcomings; which leads them towards the goal from which they are straying, and puts them back on the path they have lost. And, in the end, invariably discovers some means whereby to extricate them from the pitfalls to which the efforts and ingenuity of their blinded senses have brought them. Thus they will learn to rely solely on and submit themselves totally to God's infallible guidance. The errors into which these good souls fall cease with self-surrender, which never lets them down, for we know 'that in everything God works for good with those who love him' (Romans 8:28).

Glad Self-Surrender

Self-surrender, trust and faith, the universal means of accepting the state chosen by God's grace for each one is what I preach. To long to be the subject and instrument of divine action and to believe that it operates each moment and in all things in so far as it finds more or less good will—this is the faith I am preaching. Not a special state of grace or perfect love but a general state whereby each one of us may discover God, however he may reveal himself, and accept whatever transcendental state he has prepared for us. I have spoken to suffering souls, but now I am speaking to every kind of soul, for it is the instinctive wish of my heart to belong to all, to speak to all, to proclaim to all the good news and to be all things to all men. With this great privilege I also have a duty which I joyfully fulfil: to weep with those who are weeping, to rejoice with those who rejoice, to talk with the simple-minded in their language and to use the most erudite and learned terms with sages. I wish to make all see that everyone can aspire, not to the same specific things, but to the same love, the same surrender, the same God and his work, and thereby effortlessly achieve the most perfect saintliness. Outstanding gifts and privileges are only so called because so few souls have sufficient faith to be worthy of them. We shall see this very clearly on the day of judgement. Alas! We shall see then that it will not have been God's wish to refuse them, but through their own fault that souls will have been denied this divine mercy. What abundant rewards will total surrender have brought to a willing and a constant heart.

Responding Faithfully to Grace

With divine action it is the same as it was with Jesus. Those who did not trust or respect him never benefitted from the rewards he offered the world. Their ill will prevented them. Admittedly, all cannot hope for the same sublime state, the same gifts or the same degree of excellence. But if everyone responded faithfully to grace, each one according to his own degree, everyone would be content, because all would attain that state of perfection and privilege corresponding to and satisfying their longing. They would be content both with their natural circumstances and their state of grace, since nature and grace intermingle in the sighs which longing for that precious contentment wring from the heart.

Should we not receive the instinct appropriate to one state, we shall be given that of another. Perfect faith has its own instinct; other states have theirs. Everything in nature receives what is best suited to its kind: each flower its charm, each animal its instinct and each creature its perfection. Thus in the diversity of the states of grace each one enjoys its own special degree and there is a reward for each one whose good intention is attuned to the state in which God's care has placed them.

Love Always Prevails

As soon as their heart is willing, souls come under the influence of divine action, whose power over them depends on the extent to which they have surrendered themselves. Love is the way to this surrender. Love always prevails, is never denied. How can it be since it only asks for love in return for love? May not love long for what it gives? Divine action cares only for a willing heart and takes no account of any other faculty. Should it find a heart that is good, innocent, honest, simple, submissive, obedient and respectful, that is all it looks for. It takes possession of that heart, controls all its faculties and everything turns out so well for souls that they find themselves blessed in all things. Should what is deadly poison to other souls enter these, the antidote of their good intention never fails to counteract its effects. Should they come to the edge of an abyss, divine action turns them aside; if it lets them go, it holds them up; if they fall, it will catch them. After all, the faults of these souls are only faults of frailty and scarcely count. Love always knows how to turn them to advantage; by secret communication it indicates to them what they should say or do in every circumstance—'A good understanding have all they that do his commandments' (Psalm 110:10, Vulgate). They are flashes of divine intelligence following them everywhere, rescuing them from all the false steps they take due to their innocence. Should they get involved in bad company, God provides them with happy encounters which repair the damage. It is useless to plot and intrigue against them, he will confound the intriguers and throw them into confusion so that they fall victims of their own traps. Guided by God's purpose, those whom they wish to confound unconsciously do certain apparently senseless things, which end by delivering them from all the troubles their honesty and the malice of their enemies has brought upon them.

O what subtlety there is in this good intention! And what mystery in its virtue! Take for example the story of young Tobias and the angel. He sets out on his journey in search of a bride fearless, unfaltering, lacking nothing. His mother weeps though his father remains confident. With the angel Raphael by his side, Tobias overcomes every adversity. The very fish itself that leaps out of the water to devour him becomes his food. He thinks only of the marriage, and the divine intelligence responsible for assisting him in all things conducts his

affairs so successfully that all goes well and he returns triumphant, rejoicing to be reunited with his family.

Grant Me a Pure Heart

May others, Lord, multiply their prayers and supplications. I
ask but one thing. I offer up this prayer to you: 'Grant me a
pure heart!', O pure heart, how blessed you are! You find God
in the strength of your own faith, see him in all things, at all
times, in and around you. You are his subject and his instrument. He guides and brings you to your destination. Often you
do not think; but he is thinking for you. Whatever happens to
you is ordained by him. All he asks is your willingness. In your
bewilderment you don't understand this longing in yourself, but
he does. Ah! how simple you are! Don't you realize what a
simple heart means? It is none other than a heart where God is.
Seeing its inclination, he knows at once that there is a heart
that will always surrender itself to his command. He knows,
too, that you don't know what is for your good and makes it his
business to provide it, little caring whether you like it or not.
You are going East, he will turn you to the West. You are set
fair on a course, he turns the rudder and steers you back to
harbour. Without either compass or map, wind or tide, your
voyage is always successful; and if pirates cross your path an
unexpected gust of wind blows them off their course.

O pure and willing heart! How right Jesus was to include
you among the beatitudes. What greater bliss to possess God
and be in turn possessed by him! What enchantment, what
delight, to rest there in his arms, playing innocently, rejoicing
in divine wisdom, continuing the voyage uninterrupted over
reefs, past pirates and through continual storms without
anxiety about reaching a destination.

You Are the Spring

O pure and willing heart! The only source of all spiritual

states! It is to you that are given, and in you that blossom, the gifts of perfect faith, hope, trust and love. It is on your branches that are grafted those flowers of the desert, those precious gifts only to be seen shining in souls that are completely detached, in which God has chosen to dwell to the exclusion of all others, as though in an empty house. You are the spring whence flow all the streams which refresh the spirit. Indeed, you may tell all souls 'I am the source of true love!' Love which discovers and holds onto what is best; from which springs that sweet and powerful anxiety which inspires horror of evil, making it easier to resist; whence comes that understanding which discovers the majesty of God and the value of virtue which honours him. Love is that ardent desire, continually nourished by devout hope, which inspires the constant practice of goodness in the expectation of the divine presence. Its enjoyment will make the happiness of all faithful souls, today and for ever more. O pure of heart! You may invite them all to come and enrich themselves with your inexhaustible treasures. Every spiritual state and path leading to it, have their origin in you. All the beauty, attraction and charm they have to offer is derived from you. Those marvellous and refreshing fruits of grace and every kind of virtue shining everywhere are merely your seedlings transplanted as from a pleasure garden. It is your land that flows with milk and honey, your breast that distils the milk, in your bosom that lie the fragrant herbs and from your fingers that flows abundantly their sweet distillation.

Intoxicated in the Very Heart of God

Come, then, dear sisters, let us run, let us fly to that mother of love who is calling us. Why do we delay, why do we wait? Let us set off at once and lose and intoxicate ourselves in the very heart of God. With the key to those celestial treasures let us take the road to heaven without fear of being shut out. It will open every door. It is the key of knowledge; the key to the dark night in which are locked the profound and secret treasures of divine wisdom. It is also the key which opens the gates to mystical death, that unlocks the door to those dark and secret places into which souls are led in order that they may be rescued safe and sound. It is the key which opens the way to the happy land where dwell wisdom and light, where the mystery of love may be learned. Oh divine mystery which may not be uttered, which no mortal tongue can express!

Let us love then, dear sisters. Every gift that enriches, awaits only love. Love brings holiness and all its blessings, flooding into every heart open to its divine effulgence. O divine seed of eternity! We can never sufficiently praise you. Better to possess you in silence than praise you with feeble words. Or, rather I should say, praise we must, but let us praise you only because we are yours. For, from the moment you possess a heart it is all one whether it is reading, writing, speaking, being active or passive. In fact we are solitary or gregarious, well or ill, inarticulate or eloquent exactly according to your instructions. And in turn the heart, your faithful echo, instructs our other faculties. In this mortal and spiritual compound, this sphere which you look upon as your kingdom, it is the heart that reigns supreme under your direction. Since it has no other instincts than those inspired by you, everything you propose delights it. What human beings and the devil would like to substitute, only disgusts and horrifies the heart, and if you occasionally allow it to let itself be misled, it is only in order to make it wiser and more humble.

6. With God the More We Seem to Lose, the More We Gain

Understanding Divine Action

Let us pursue our understanding of divine action further. What it appears to take from good will it replaces, as it were, incognito, never allowing good will to suffer any loss. It is as though someone let it be known that he was assisting a friend financially and, while continuing to do so, were to pretend, for the friend's benefit, to withdraw his help. The friend, not suspecting this strategy or understanding the mystery of love, would feel deeply hurt. But how mistaken he would be! What a reproach to his benefactor's generosity! However, once the mystery clarifies, God knows all the joy, tenderness, gratitude, love, embarrassment and admiration that will fill his soul. Will he not have a greater warmth and admiration for his benefactor, will it not strengthen his trust in him and guard against similar misunderstandings in the future? The implication is clear. With God, the more we seem to lose, the more we gain. The more he takes materially, the more he gives spiritually. We love him partly for his gifts. If they are no longer visible we come to love him for himself alone. It is by seeming to deprive us of those gifts that he paves the way for his most precious one of all, because it embraces everything. Souls, once they have totally surrendered themselves

to his action, see everything that happens to them in a favourable light, be it the loss of an excellent director, or the vague
mistrust they may have of any who volunteer advice too
freely—though the kind of directors who pursue souls unin-
vited are often somewhat suspect. Those who are truly led by
the Holy Spirit are not normally so pressing and conceited,
and rarely offer advice unasked and, if they do, offer it reluc-
tantly.

Listen to the Heart

However, to come back to these souls. Their heart may be
said to be the interpreter of God's word. Listen to the heart, it
interprets his will in everything that happens. For divine
action secretly informs the heart of its purpose through the
instincts rather than through the mind, indicating them either
by chance happenings making the heart respond at random, or
through necessity in which case there is no choice, or through
impulses to which there is an instinctive response. For example,
when something is said or done on the spur of the moment, or
in a moment of transcendental ecstasy; or, again, through
some strong attraction or aversion whereby souls are drawn to
or repelled by certain objects.

It is like a musician who combines long practice with a perfect understanding of music, who is so immersed in his art that
everything he undertakes connected with it will have a touch
of this perfection. If his composition were to be examined, it
would turn out that they conformed perfectly to the conventions and that he was most successful when working unham-
pered by them—so much so, that connoisseurs would hail his
impromptus as masterpieces. For conventions, if followed too
closely, restrict talent.

Thus those experienced in the skill and practice of sanctity,
with understanding and method in addition to grace, unconsciously form the habit which becomes second nature, of

acting on intuition and faith in all things. It turns out then, that they can do no better than to act on impulse, without spending hours of thought on what they are going to do beforehand as they used to. All they have to do is to act as though by chance, trusting only to the power of grace which can never be wrong. What they achieve in this state of innocence and trust is nothing short of a miracle to eyes that can see and minds that can perceive. Without rules, nothing more orderly; without preparation, nothing better planned; without thought, nothing more profound; without skill, nothing more accomplished; without effort, nothing more effective; and without precaution, nothing better adjusted to whatever may happen.

Nevertheless, souls find themselves at a loss in this state, without the help of the insight or discrimination which used to guide and direct all they did, or of grace which no longer manifests itself. But it is in this very loss that they rediscover everything, since that same grace, taking upon itself a new form, repays them a hundredfold for what it has taken from them by the perfection of its hidden influence.

No doubt it is mortifying for souls to lose sight of the divine will which vanishes from view only in order to get behind them, so to speak, and to push them along, becoming no longer an aim but a motive. Experience shows that nothing sets alight in the heart a longing for that will so much as its loss. The heart sighs deeply for it and cannot be comforted.

Wonderful Mystery of Love

Wonderful mystery of love! To deprive a heart of God that longs only for him! For by this means alone can perfect faith be established in souls. Then it is that they will believe what they cannot see and rely on what they cannot grasp with their senses. What perfection comes from this mysterious influence whose subject and instrument we are, and of whose existence we are not even conscious so much does it seem to be part of what we do of our own accord! What humiliation overwhelms souls when, inspired by God to speak, they think they are doing so of their own free will. Never knowing what is urging them on, the most divine impulses trouble them. Despising all they do, they admire what is done by others and feel themselves to be far inferior. To rely on their own efforts to overcome these apparent faults is futile, for they are God's admirable plan to force them to depend entirely on his help.

How mysterious are the ways of divine action! To sanctify souls in the semblance of nothing but humiliation! This truly wonderful, divine and exceptional sanctity can only grow out of humility! Nor do the fruits of such perfect faith ever perish for their husk is too dry and hard.

God's Secret Hiding Place

So may this seed germinate in your heart, God's secret hiding place, and through his mysterious virtue throw out branches, leaves, flowers and fruit which you cannot see but by which others will be nourished and enchanted. Give all who seek rest and refreshment in your shade fruits to their liking regardless of your own, and may each of your branches bear only the marks of grace. Be everything to all men and remain submissive and indifferent yourself. Exist little worm, in the dark confines of your narrow cocoon, until the warmth of grace hatches you out. Then devour the leaves offered you, and, forgetting the quietude you have abandoned, surrender yourself to this activity, until divine nature stops you. Alternatively active and passive, by incomprehensible transformations, lose your former self, manner and habits, and through death and resurrection, assume those which divine nature will herself choose for you. Then spin your silk in secret, unconscious of what you are doing, inwardly dissatisfied with yourself, envying your companions who are dead and at peace, admiring them even though they never reached your degree of perfection. By surrendering yourself you will be inspired to spin silk that princes of the Church and of the state, and fine ladies, will be proud to wear. And then what will become of you? Where will you go? O miracle of grace! Whereby souls discover so many different forms! Who knows where grace may lead them? Who could ever have guessed what nature makes of a silk worm unless they had seen it! Only give it leaves, nature does the rest.

And so, dear sisters, you will never know either from whence you come or where you are going, from what purpose of God divine wisdom has taken you and to where it is leading you. All that remains for you to do is passively to surrender yourselves, offering no resistance, without thought, aim, guidance or direction, acting when it is the moment to act, ceasing when it is the moment to cease, losing when it is the moment to lose; and thus, active or passive, eager or indifferent, reading, writing, talking or silent, never knowing what is going to happen next. And, after many transformations, perfected, your souls will receive wings to fly up to heaven, having sown on earth the fertile seed of their state of self-surrender to live in others for ever.

7. The Mystery of God's Grace

The Mystery of the Perfected Soul

God's order, his pleasure, his will, his action and grace, all these are one and the same. The purpose on earth of this divine power is perfection. It is formed, grows and is accomplished secretly in souls without their knowledge. Theology is full of theories and arguments expounding the miracles it works in each soul. We may be able to understand all these speculations, cogently discuss, write, teach and instruct souls through them. But with only this in mind, in relation to those in whom that divine purpose exists, I suggest we are like sick doctors trying to cure patients in perfect health. God's order and his divine will, humbly obeyed by the faithful, accomplishes this divine purpose in them without their knowledge, in the same way as medicine obediently swallowed cures invalids who neither know nor care how. Just as it is fire and not the philosophy or science of that element and its effects that heats, so it is God's order and his will which sanctify and not curious speculations about its origin or purpose.

To quench thirst it is necessary to drink. Reading books about it only makes it worse. Thus, when we long for sanctity, speculation only drives it further from our grasp. We must humbly accept all that God's order requires us to do and suffer. What he ordains for us each moment is what is most holy, best and most divine for us.

All we need to know is how to recognize his will in the present moment. Grace is the will of God and his order acting in the centre of our hearts when we read or are occupied in other ways; theories and studies, without regard for the refreshing virtue of God's order, are merely dead letters, emptying the heart by filling the mind. This divine will flowing through the soul of a simple uneducated girl, through her suffering or some exceptionally noble act in adversity, carries out in her heart God's mysterious purpose, without a thought entering her head. Whereas the sophisticated man, who studies spiritual books out of mere curiosity, whose reading is not inspired by God, takes into his mind only dead letters and grows even more arid and obtuse.

God's order or his divine will is the life of all souls who either seek or obey it.

In whatever way this divine will may benefit the mind, it nourishes the soul. These blessed results are not produced by any particular circumstance but by what God ordains for the present moment. What was best a moment ago is so no longer because it is removed from the divine will, which has passed on to be changed to form the duty to the next. And it is that duty, whatever it may be, that is now most sanctifying for the soul.

Establishing Jesus in Our Heart

If the divine will ordains that reading is the duty to the present moment, reading achieves that mysterious purpose. If the divine will abandons reading for an act of contemplation, that duty will bring about a change of heart and then reading will be harmful and useless. If the divine will rejects contemplation for confessions and the like (especially if they are lengthy), it will establish Jesus Christ in our heart which all the sweetness of contemplation would only prevent.

The mysterious growth of Jesus Christ in our heart is the accomplishment of God's purpose, the fruit of his grace and divine will. This fruit, as has been pointed out, forms, grows, and ripens in the succession of our duties to the present which are continually being replenished by God, so that obeying them is always the best we can do. We must offer no resistance, and blindly abandon ourselves to his divine will in perfect trust. This divine will is infinitely wise, powerful and benevolent towards souls who totally and unreservedly put their trust in it, and who love and seek it alone, and who believe with an unshakeable faith and confidence that what the divine will ordains each moment is best, who look no further afield for vain comparisons with any material benefits God's order may bring.

The will of God is the presence, the reality and the virtue in all things, adjusting them to souls. Without God's direction all is void, emptiness, vanity, words, superficiality, death. The will of God is the salvation, sanity and life of body and soul whatever else it may bring to either of them. Whether it be vexation and trouble for the mind, or sickness and death for the body, nevertheless that divine will remains all in all. Bread without the divine will is poison, with it true sustenance. Without the divine will reading only blinds and perplexes, with it it enlightens. The divine will is the wholeness, the good and the true in all things. Like God, the universal Being, it is manifest in everything. It is not necessary to look to the benefits received by the mind and body to judge of their virtue. These are of no significance. It is the will of God that gives everything, whatever it may be, the power to form Jesus Christ in the centre of our being. This will knows no limits.

The True and Only Virtue
Divine action does not distinguish between creatures, whether they are useless or useful. Without it everything is nothing, with it nothing is everything. Whether contemplation, meditation, prayer, inward silence, intuition, quietude or activity are

what we wish for ourselves, the best is God's purposes for us at the present moment. Souls must look upon everything as though it were a matter of complete indifference, and seeing only him in all things must take or leave them as he wishes, so as to live, be nourished by and hope in him alone and not by any power or virtue which does not come from him. Every moment, and in respect of everything, they must say, like St Paul, 'Lord what should I do?' Let me do everything you wish. The spirit wants one thing the body another, but Lord, I wish only to do your divine will. Supplication, intercession, mental or vocal prayer, action or silence, faith or wisdom, particular sacraments or general grace, all these, Lord, are nothing, for your purpose is the true and only virtue in all things. It alone, and nothing else, however sublime or exalted, is the object of my devotion since the purpose of grace is the perfection of the heart not of the mind.

The presence of God which sanctifies our souls is the Holy Trinity which dwells in our hearts when they surrender to the divine will. God's presence coming to us through an act of contemplation brings about this secret union. Like everything else belonging to God's order and enjoined by the divine will, it must always take first place as the most perfect means of uniting ourselves to God.

It is by being united to the will of God that we enjoy and possess him, and it is a delusion to seek this divine possession by any other means. Being united to God is the only way, not in any specific manner or style, but in a thousand different ways, and the one he chooses for us is the best. But they must all be loved and esteemed, since they are all ordained by God and his purpose, chosen for and adapted to each soul to bring about the divine union. And souls must abide by his choice, preferring the way of this blessed will and must love and respect it just as much in others. For example, if God's purpose prescribes vocal prayers, loving sentiments, insight into the mysteries for me, I must love and respect the silence and bareness which a life of faith inspires in others. But for myself, I must make use of my duty to the present, and by it unite myself to God. I must not, like the quietists, reduce all religion to a denial of any specific action, despising all other means, since what makes perfection is God's order, and the means he ordains is best for the soul. No, we must set no bounds or limits or shape to the will of God. We must accept any way he chooses to communicate with us, and respect any way it pleases him to unite himself to others. Thus, all simple souls have but one general way, though specific and different in each one, which makes up the diversity of the mystical experience. All simple souls must admire and respect one another, saying: 'Let us proceed each one along our path to the same goal, united in purpose and by means of God's order which, in its great variety, is in us all.' It is in this light that the lives of the saints and the mystical books must be read, without ever being misled or going astray. It is why it is absolutely essential neither to read nor hold spiritual discourse unless ordained by God. Since his order makes it their duty to the present to do so, far from being misled, souls will find reassurance in the very things which contradict what they have learnt. But if God's order does not make this reading and spiritual discourse the duty to the present moment, they will always emerge troubled and find themselves confused and uncertain. Without God there can be no order anywhere. How long, then, shall we continue to concern ourselves with our own liberty or our own capacity to suffer the trials and tribulations of the present moment? When will God be all in all to us? Let us see things in their true light and rise above them to live purely in God himself.

This Diet of Dust and Ashes
This is why God spreads so much desolation, emptiness, obscurity and humiliation over everything that happens to certain

souls. Their suffering seems trivial and despicable in their own as well as in the eyes of others; it is commonplace, inglorious. Trouble inwardly, contradiction and frustration outwardly; a frail body exposed to many hardships experiencing the drawbacks of poverty and deprivation for which saints are admired. No sign of lavish almsgiving, or burning zeal. With such an unappetising diet, in so far as the body and mind are concerned, are souls nourished. And, since none of this satisfies them, they aspire to other things only to find that every avenue to the salvation they so earnestly long for is closed. To eat humble pie, this diet of dust and ashes, requires an inward and outward discipline, and a steadfast and implacable conception of what sanctification means. The will is starving for it, but these souls find no means of attaining it. Why all this, if not in order that they may be mortified by what is most spiritual and inward? Finding neither appetite for nor satisfaction in anything that happens to them, they put all their hope in God who is leading them along this path in order that he alone shall please them. Let us abandon, then, the outer husk of our painful life, since it only humiliates us both in our own and in the eyes of others. Or rather let us hide behind it and rejoice in God who is our only good. Let us make use of our frailty, hardships, these cares, this need for food and clothing and possessions, these failures, suspicion of others, these doubts and anxieties, these perplexities, and find our joy in God who, through them, gives himself wholly to us to be our only blessing.

God wishes to dwell in us in poverty without any of the trappings for which we win so much praise. All he wishes is to be the sole object and only enchantment of our hearts. And we are so frail that if this meant the glamour of self-denial, zeal, almsgiving and poverty we should make it all part of our delight. However, we find in our path nothing that is not disagreeable and so we turn to God, our only blessing and prop. Let the world despise us and leave us in peace to rejoice in our own special riches.

God wants to be the source of everything in us that is holy, and for that reason everything that depends on ourselves and on our personal faith is insignificant and quite the opposite of saintliness.

We can never achieve anything great except through surrendering ourselves; therefore let us think no more about it. Let us leave the care of our salvation to God. He knows the way. It is under the special protection and guidance of his concern for us, acting often in ways unknown to us and even through what we most fear and least expect. Let us march on in the trivial duties of our personal devotion without aspiring to great ones, for God does not wish to manifest himself through our own efforts. We shall be God's saints through his grace and special providence. He has his plans for us, so leave it to him. Henceforth, without entertaining vain thoughts and false ideas about sanctity, let us be content to love him unceasingly and walk humbly in the path he has marked out for us, where all seems so trivial in our own and in the eyes of the world.

8. The Sacrament of the Present Moment: The Soul's Part

Boundless Submission

'Sacrifice a just sacrifice and hope in the Lord' (Psalm 4:8, Vulgate) said the prophet.

That is to say that the sure and solid foundation of our spiritual life is to give ourselves to God and put ourselves entirely in his hands body and soul. To forget ourselves completely so that he becomes our whole joy and his pleasure and glory, his being, our only good. To think of ourselves as objects sold and delivered, for God to do with what he likes.

With this foundation laid, souls have but to spend their entire existence rejoicing that God is God, surrendering themselves so completely that they are happy to obey his commands whatever they may be and without question.

God uses his creatures in two ways. Either he makes them act on their own initiative or he himself acts through them. The first requires a faithful fulfilment of his manifest wishes; the second, a meek and humble submission to his inspiration. Surrender of self achieves them both, being nothing more than a total commitment to the word of God within the present moment. It is not important for his creatures to know how they must do this or what the nature of the present moment is.

What is absolutely essential is an unreserved surrender of themselves.

A contrite and submissive heart opens the way to pleasing God. An ecstasy of perfect love pervades the fulfilment of his will by those who surrender to it; and this surrender practised each moment embodies every kind of virtue and excellence. It is not for us to determine what manner of submission we owe to God, but only humbly to submit to and be ready to accept everything that comes to us. The rest is up to him. And whether we take pains to fulfil the task to which our circumstances and duty call us, or whether we meekly follow inspired inclination, or obediently submit to the exigencies of grace for body and soul, in all this we are achieving in the heart the same universal act of submission unconcerned about the particular purpose or consequence. With this total indifference to results, such acts have essentially all the merit and value good intentions always have, for in the eyes of God they always achieve their purpose. And even if God wishes to limit some of our faculties he never limits our good intentions. God's purpose, the being and essence of God, becomes the object of these intentions and God unites himself to them in love without stint or measure. And if that eternal love partly ends in the senses it is because God's will does too. By reducing itself, as it were, to the dimensions of the present moment, it is able to reach the senses and from there pass into the heart. God can then communicate with the heart because, having been emptied of everything by the infinite power of his perfect love, the heart is pure and undefiled and so redeemed and made fit to receive him.

O holy redemption, it is you that prepares the way for God! O perfection! O boundless submission, it is you that draws God deep into the heart! Let the senses feel what they may, you, Lord, are all my good! Do what you like to this tiny being, let it act, be inspired, be the object of your purpose! I have nothing more to see or do, not a single moment of my life is in my own hands. All is yours, I have nothing to add, remove, seek or consider. It is for you to direct everything. Sanctification, perfection, salvation, guidance and humility are your responsibility. Mine is to be content, dispassionate, passive, leaving everything to your pleasure.

The Doctrine of Perfect Love

The doctrine of perfect love comes to us through God's action alone and not through our own efforts. God instructs the heart, not through ideas but through suffering and adversity. To know this is to understand that God is our only good. To achieve it it is necessary to be indifferent to all material blessings, and to arrive at this point one must be deprived of them all. Thus it is only through continual affliction, misfortune and a long succession of mortifications of every kind to our feelings and affections that we are established in perfect love. The point must be reached when the whole of creation counts for nothing and God for everything. This is the reason why God opposes all our personal inclinations and ideas. No sooner do we form our own ideas or notions of piety or means to perfection or whatever designs we may have, or advice we may take, God disconcerts all our plans and instead permits us to find in them only confusion, trouble, vanity and folly. Scarcely do we tell ourselves 'This is the way, this is who to ask, what to do!', then no sooner does God say exactly the opposite and withdraws his virtue from the decisions we have made. And so, discovering in everything only mortality and consequently nothingness, we are forced to turn to God himself to find our happiness in him.

Souls to whom God's good pleasure has become their own are no longer suffused with mystical love. Obedient to God's command and the special fulfilment of his will, and resigned to their human condition, they exist oblivious of both its joys and

[51]

sorrows in the fulness of God's enduring mercy. He finds these souls sunk in apathy and takes possession of their heart. Living in God in this way the heart is dead to all else and all else is dead to it. For it is God alone who gives life to all things, who quickens the soul in the creature and the creature in the soul. God's word is that life. With it the heart and the creature are one. Without it they are strangers. Without the virtue of the divine will all creation is reduced to nothing, with it, it is brought into the realm of his kingdom where every moment is complete contentment in God alone, and a total surrender of all creatures to his order. It is the sacrament of the present moment.

Surrender and Assent

The practice of this excellent theology is so simple, so easy and so accessible that it need only be wished for it to be had. This indifference, this love so perfect, so universal, is both active and passive, in so far as what we do through grace, and what grace accomplishes in us, requires nothing more than surrender and assent. In fact it is everything that God himself ordains and mystical theology expounds in a multitude of subtle concepts which it is often better for us not to know, since all that is required is oblivion and surrender.

It is enough, then, for us to know what we must do, and this is the easiest thing in the world. It is to love God as the mighty all in all, to rejoice in him and to fulfil our duty conscientiously and wisely. Simple souls who follow this path, so straight, so clear and so safe, have only to walk with guarded step in confidence, and all the admirable propositions of mystical theology, which involve tribulation and inward grace, are carried out, unnoticed by them, through God's will. While they think only of loving and obeying him, his will operates in a way that the more committed souls are, the more withdrawn and detached from everything in themselves, the more perfectly the work is accomplished; whereas their own opinions, searching, and cleverness can only be opposed to the way God acts in which lies all their good. He sanctifies, purifies, guides, enlightens and makes them useful to others. He makes them his apostles by ways and means which seem to point to the contrary.

Everything in the present moment tends to draw us away from the path of love and passive obedience. It requires heroic courage and self-surrender to hold firmly to a simple faith and to keep singing the same tune confidently while grace itself seems to be singing a different one in another key, giving us the impression that we have been misled and are lost. But if only we have the courage to let the thunder, lightning and storm rage, and to walk unfaltering in the path of love and obedience to the duty and demands of the present moment, we are emulating Jesus himself. For we are sharing that passion during which our Saviour walked with equal firmness and courage in the love of his father and in obedience to his will, submitting to treatment which seemed utterly opposed to the dignity of so holy a saint.

Jesus and Mary, on that dark night, let the storm break over them, a deluge which, in apparent opposition to God's will, harms them. They march undaunted in the path of love and obedience, keeping their eyes on what they have to do, and leaving God to do what he will. They groan under the weight of that divine action, but do not falter or stop for a single moment, believing that all will be well providing they keep on their course and leave the rest to God.

The Reverse Side of the Tapestry

All goes well when God is, so to speak, both the author and the object of our faith, the one complementing and augmenting the other. It is like the right side of a beautiful tapestry being worked stitch by stitch on the reverse side. Neither the stitches nor the needle are visible, but, one by one, those stitches make a magnificent pattern that only becomes apparent when the work is completed and the right side exposed to the light of day; although while it is in progress there is no sign of its beauty and wonder.

The same applies to self-surrendered souls who see only God and their duty. The accomplishment of that duty is at each moment one imperceptible stitch added to the tapestry. And yet it is with these stitches that God performs wonders of which one occasionally has a presentiment at the time, but which will not be fully known until the great day of judgement. How wise and bountiful are the works of God! He reserves for himself, his grace and his action, all that is sublime, magnificent and glorious in perfection and holiness; and leaves to us, with the help of grace, all that is straightforward, simple and easy, so that there is no one in the world who cannot easily attain to the highest degree of perfection. Everything connected with surrender of self, devotion to duty or purity is attainable by every Christian. Excluding only sin, that is all God requires for the achievement of perfect faith. All he expects is the fulfilment of his will, as signified by our duty to the present moment to be as faithful as we can to our obligations so far as it is in our spiritual and temporal powers to do so. What could be easier or more reasonable? How can we plead to be let off? For this is all that God requires of us for the accomplishment of our sanctification whether we are strong or weak, great or small. In a word, from all, at all times and in all places. And it is indeed true that he is only asking from us what is easy and simple, since this basic foundation is sufficient on which to build the most perfect holiness.

What Is Our Duty?

What, then, is this duty which for each one of us is the very essence of our perfection? It is twofold: a general obligation which God imposes on all mankind; and specific obligations which he prescribes for each individual. God involves each one in different circumstances in which to carry out his purpose. He binds us to his love and influences our purpose so that it may become the object of his grace, showing his mercy by asking from each one no more than he is able to give.

O you who reach after perfection and are tempted to be discouraged by what you read about the lives of the saints and what works of piety prescribe! Who are daunted by exalted notions of perfection! It is for your consolation that God wishes me to write this. Know what you seem to be unaware of: that God in his mercy has made free everything which is necessary for human existence, such as air, water and earth. Nothing is more essential than breathing, sleeping and eating, yet nothing is more available. In accordance with God's commandment, love and faith are no less essential and common to our spiritual needs, and so the difficulties cannot be so great as we imagine. Even in things of little consequence, God is easily satisfied by the part souls are to play in the achievement of their perfection. He himself is too explicit for us to doubt it. 'Fear God, and keep his commandments; for this is the whole duty of man' (Ecclesiastes 12:13). Which is to say, that is all men must do for their part; it is their living faith. Let them do it, God will do the rest. Grace alone will perform the miracles passing the understanding of men, for the ear has not heard nor the eye seen nor the heart felt, what God conceives in his mind, resolves in his will and by his power performs in souls (1 Corinthians 2:9). We present this simple background, this picture so clear, these colours so evenly applied, this composition so admirable, so skilfully perfected. The hand of divine wisdom alone knows how to cover this canvas of love and obedience which souls unconsciously hold up, unquestioning and without bothering to find out what God is adding to it because, trusting and surrendering themselves to him, they are only concerned with doing their duty and think neither about themselves nor what their needs are nor how to obtain them.

Let God's Will Be Done

The more they work at their humble task, however lowly and obscure it may be outwardly, the more God adorns, embellishes and enriches it with the colours he adds. 'The Lord has made excellent he who is faithful to him' (Psalm 4:4, Vulgate).

Is not a picture painted on a canvas by the application of one stroke of the brush at a time? Similarly the cruel chisel destroys a stone with each cut. But what the stone suffers by repeated blows is no less than the shape the mason is making of it. And should a poor stone be asked 'What is happening to you?', it might reply 'Don't ask me. All I know is that for my part there is nothing for me to know or do, only to remain steady under the hand of my master and to love him and suffer him to work out my destiny. It is for him to know how to achieve this. I know neither what he is doing nor why. I only know that he is doing what is best and most perfect, and I suffer each cut of the chisel as though it were the best thing for me, even though, to tell the truth, each one is my idea of ruin, destruction and defacement. But, ignoring all this, I rest contented with the present moment. Thinking only of my duty to it, I submit to the work of this skilful master without caring to know what it is.'

Yes, dear sisters, simple souls, leave to God what belongs to him, and go your way in peace and quiet! Let God's will be done and surrender yourselves to him! Let the chisel and the needle and the brush do their work, seeing in all this great diversity merely the wash of colour suitable for daubing your canvas. Respond to these divine operations meekly and obediently, remembering only to do your duty. Follow your path without a map, not knowing the way, and all will be revealed to you. Seek only God's kingdom and his justice through love and obedience, and all will be granted to you. Many will ask anxiously, 'Where shall we find holiness, perfection, humility and wisdom?' Let them ask, let them search in books for the purpose and merit of this marvellous operation, its nature and aim.

Remain at peace yourselves, united to God in love, and continue blindly along the straight and narrow path of duty.

The angels are beside you in this dark night, their arms around you. Should God require more of you he will make it known. God's order gives everything a super-natural and divine quality. Everything he touches, everything he reveals, every object over which he sheds his light, are made holy and perfect since his virtue knows no bounds. To have this touch of holiness and not to stray away from it, it is necessary for souls to consider whether or not the inspiration they believe comes from God conflicts with the duty of their state, and if it does, to remember that it is God's order that must prevail. There is nothing to fear or reject, no choice to be made. The most precious and purifying moment for souls is to be certain that they are accomplishing God's will.

All saints become saints by fulfilling those duties themselves to which they have been called. It is not by the things they do, their nature or particular qualities that holiness must be judged. It is obeying those orders which sanctifies souls and enlightens, or purifies and humbles, them. And so all the virtue in what we call holiness lies in this order of God, and therefore there is nothing to be lost or gained; there is only to accept everything that comes from him and nothing that does not. Books, sage advice, vocal prayers, personal affection, all instruct, direct and unite us if ordained by God. It is in vain for quietism to reject these and all tangible means of direction, for there are souls whom God wishes to follow that path, and their state and inclination make this quite clear. It is useless to dream of ways to surrender ourselves in which all effort of our own is rejected and total quietude sought, for if God ordains that we should achieve certain things ourselves, surrendering ourselves consists in doing these things. Our own decisions will be in vain and our surrender to God more perfect. For some souls, this command is limited to the duties of their state in life and the passive acceptance of God's will. That is what is most perfect for them. For others, apart from this, there are besides several other special duties over and above those of their state in life. Intuition and inspiration are then the intimations of God's will and it is best for souls to obey them, not forgetting, however, the caution required when doing so. And to imagine that these souls are more or less perfect merely because their duties are more exalted, is to place perfection, not in surrender to God's will, but in the duties themselves. God makes his saints as he pleases. It is by his command that they are made, and all are subject to it. This is true surrender; it is the height of perfection.

True Surrender

Duty to their state in life and to God's purpose is common to all saints; it is his general direction for them all. These souls live unnoticed in obscurity, avoiding the pitfalls of the world. This is not what makes them saints, but the more they surrender to God the more saintly they become. It does not however follow that those in whom God manifests virtues by remarkable and outstanding actions, or through obedience to divinely inspired inclinations and intuitions, follow the path of surrender any the less. For they would not be surrendered to God and to his will, nor would every moment of their lives be governed by it, nor would God be in each moment, if they were merely content with the duty to their state and obedient to divine providence. These souls must stretch and measure themselves according to God's purpose for them, as indicated by intuition and inspiration which must be faithfully obeyed. And, just as there are souls whose whole duty is indicated by an external law to which they are bound by God's will to conform, there are others who, in addition, must also obey that inner law engraved on their heart by the Holy Spirit.

[58]

It is mere idle curiosity to ask which of them is more saintly. Each one must follow his allotted path. Saintliness consists in submitting to the will of God, and all the perfection to be found in it. Further searching does not help us, since it is not in the quality or quantity of our obligations that we must look for saintliness. If self-love inspires our actions or if it is not corrected as soon as it appears, we shall always be poor in a plenty which lacks God's bounty. However, on reflection, I believe that saintliness depends on the measure of love we have for the will of God; and that the more we love it, whatever it may be, the greater is also our saintliness. And this is borne out by Jesus, Mary and Joseph, since in their private lives there was more nobility and excellence than worldly splendour, and we never say of that Holy Family that they looked for the holiness of things but only the holiness within things. And all this shows that there is no one particular or specific way which is the most perfect, but that perfection is to be found in surrendering to the will of God, each one according to his state and circumstance.

The Third Duty Required of Souls

The first duty required of souls is self-discipline; the second is self-surrender and complete passivity; the third requires great humility, a humble and willing disposition and a readiness to follow the movement of grace which motivates everything if they simply respond willingly to all its guidance. And in order that souls should not lose their way, God never fails to provide them with wise directors to show how much freedom and how much restraint will be best for them. And this third duty truly supersedes every law, every formula and every established custom. It inspires in souls unique and remarkable resolutions and governs their vocal prayers, their inner voice, the perception of their senses and the radiance of their lives. It is what gives them their self-denial, their fervour, their prodigal devotion to their neighbour. And, since this is the unique gift of the Holy Spirit, no one should dare to prescribe it for himself, or aspire to it, or lament that he has not the grace to enable him to achieve these rare virtues which are only acquired under God's auspices. Otherwise, as had already been pointed out, there is a danger of being deluded. We must remember that there are souls whom God wishes to keep hidden, humble and obscure in their own eyes as well as in the eyes of others. For whom, far from ordaining such conspicuous virtue, which they would be well advised not to aspire to, God has quite different plans. They must faithfully follow their path, finding peace in their humility. The only difference in their way is in their love and surrender to God's will. Because, since they surpass in humility souls who seem outwardly to be more devoted to their duty, who can doubt that they are more saintly? Thus all must be content with the duties to their state and to God's direction. He clearly demands this. As for the strong impressions and inspirations souls receive, they must not judge them themselves nor exaggerate their importance. Conscious effort is directly contrary to inspired action; this only comes through peace and serenity. For it is the voice of God waking souls who are only able to act when the Spirit moves them and can do nothing on their own. Though they may not be moved by grace to do all those marvels which make saints so admired, they can justly say: 'God asks this of saints, but not of me.'

I believe if they were so to behave they would spare themselves a great deal of trouble. And the same is true of worldly people. If the former knew what work was to be done each moment, I mean their daily tasks and duties; if the latter could only appreciate the things they disregard and even consider useless and irrelevant to the holiness of which they have formed such exalted ideas; if they knew that those ideas, though perhaps good in themselves, were always harmful because they are limited to our human conception of what is splendid and marvellous; if all knew that saintliness consists of all the suffering which their state provides each moment; that it is not any exceptional state that leads to the sublime heights of perfection; that the philosopher's stone is surrender to God's will which makes everything they do divine—how happy they would be! How clearly they would see that to be a saint there is no more to do than what they are doing, and no more to suffer than what they are suffering; that even what they reject and count for nothing would be enough to purchase the most blessed holiness.

How I long to be the missionary of your divine will, O God, to teach the world that there is nothing easier, more ordinary, more available to all than saintliness. Just as there was no difference between what the good and the bad thief had to do and suffer in order to become saints, neither is there for souls, some of whom are worldly and others spiritual. Those who damn their souls do so by attempting to achieve through their fantasies what those who save their souls achieve through submitting to your will, and by protesting and grumbling about what those who are saved suffer with resignation. Thus, only the heart is different.

Dear sisters who read this! Do what you are doing, suffer what you are suffering, only your heart need be changed. It will cost you nothing, for this change only consists in desiring everything that God ordains. Yes, holiness is a will disposed to conform to God's. And what can be easier? Since who can resist adoring a will so loving and so good? This love alone makes everything divine.

9. The Secret of Discovering God's Transcendent Will in the Present Moment

The Present Moment Holds Infinite Riches

Nothing is more reasonable, perfect or divine than the will of God. No difference in time, place or circumstance could add to its infinite worth, and if you have been granted the secret of how to discover it in every moment, you have found what is most precious and desirable. God is telling you, dear sisters, that if you abandon all restraint, carry your wishes to their furthest limits, open your heart boundlessly, there is not a single moment when you will not be shown everything you can possibly wish for.

The present moment holds infinite riches beyond your wildest dreams but you will only enjoy them to the extent of your faith and love. The more a soul loves, the more it longs, the more it hopes, the more it finds. The will of God is manifest in each moment, an immense ocean which the heart only fathoms in so far as it overflows with faith, trust and love. The whole of the rest of creation cannot fill your heart, which is larger than all that is not God; terrifying mountains are mere molehills to it. It is in his purpose, hidden in the cloud of all that happens to you in the present moment, that you must rely. You will find it always surpasses your own wishes. Woo no man, worship no shadows or fantasies; they have nothing to offer or accept from you. Only God's purpose can satisfy your longing and leave you nothing to wish for. Adore, walk close to it, see through and abandon all fantasy. Faith is death and destruction to the senses for they worship creatures, whereas faith worships the divine will of God. Discard idols, and the senses will cry like disappointed children, but faith triumphs for it can never be estranged from God's will. When the present moment terrifies, crushes, lays waste and over-whelms the senses, God nourishes, strengthens and revives faith, which, like a general in command of an impregnable position, scorns such useless defences.

When the will of God is revealed to souls and has made them feel that they, for their part, have given themselves to him, they are aware of a powerful ally on every hand, for then they taste the happiness of the presence of God which they can only enjoy when they have learnt, through surrendering themselves, where they stand each moment in relation to his ever-loving will.

Recognizing God in the Most Trivial

Do not imagine that these souls judge things like those who judge them with their senses and who are unaware of the in-estimable treasures they hold. He who recognizes a king in disguise treats him very differently from he who sees before him only the figure of an ordinary man and treats him accordingly. Likewise, souls who can recognize God in the most trivial, the most grievous and the most mortifying things that happen to them in their lives, honour everything equally with delight and rejoicing, and welcome with open arms what others dread and avoid. The senses despise mean trappings but the heart worships this royal majesty in whatever form it appears, and the more humble its disguise the more the heart is pierced through with love. How can what the heart feels be described when it perceives God's divine word so shrunken, so beggarly, so prostrated? Ah! The poverty, the humility of God reduced to lying on straw in a manger, crying and trembling and breaking Mary's noble heart. Ask the inhabitants of Bethlehem what they think; if that child had been born in a palace in princely surroundings they would worship him. But ask Mary, Joseph, the Magi, the priests, and they will tell you that they see in this dire poverty something which makes God more glorious, more adorable. What is deprivation to the senses nourishes and strengthens faith. The less there is for them, the more there is for the soul.

To adore Jesus at the transfiguration, to love God in great things, is not so perfect an act of faith as to worship them in small ones, to worship Jesus on the cross, since faith is only truly living when what is seen and felt, deny and try to destroy it. Perfect faith emerges from this battle with the senses strengthened and triumphant.

To discover God in the smallest and most ordinary things, as well as in the greatest, is to possess a rare and sublime faith. To find contentment in the present moment is to relish and adore the divine will in the succession of all the things to be done and suffered which make up the duty to the present moment. The pure of heart, simple souls, worship God in all the most adverse circumstances; their faith triumphs over everything. The more their senses tell them 'God is not there', the more they drain this cup of bitterness; nothing dismays them, nothing repels them. It was Mary who remained at the foot of the cross when the Apostles fled, and who recognized her son when he was disfigured, spat upon and bruised. It only made him more beloved in the eyes of that tender mother; the more he was blasphemed, the greater her veneration for him. A living faith is nothing else than a steadfast pursuit of God through all that disguises, disfigures, demolishes and seeks, so to speak, to abolish him.

To go back to Mary. When all the world disowned, abandoned and persecuted her son, she followed him from the stable to Calvary. In the same way faithful souls triumph over a succession of mortifications, shadows and fantasies which contrive to make God's purpose unrecognizable, and pursue and adore it to the very foot of the cross. All know that they must always abandon the shadows to follow that sublime sun which, from dawn to dusk, however heavy and dark the clouds which hide it, illuminates, warms and inspires whoever bless, worship and gaze in wonder on every point of its mysterious circumference. Then run, faithful souls, happy and tireless, keep up with your beloved who marches with giant strides from one end of heaven to the other. Nothing is hidden from his eyes. He walks alike over the smallest blade of grass, the tallest cedars, grains of sand or rocky mountains. Wherever you go he has gone before. Only follow him and you will find him everywhere.

The Living Word

God's written word is full of mystery; his word accomplished on earth is none the less so. These are truly closed books whose words annihilate reason. God is the fount of faith, a dark abyss from whose depths faith flows. All his words, all his works are, so to speak, only dim rays of that even more remote sun. We open our bodily eyes to see the sun and its rays, but the eyes of our soul, through which we see God and his works, are sightless. For here darkness takes the place of light, knowledge is ignorance, and not seeing we see. Holy Scripture is the mysterious word of a God even more mysterious, and the events of time are the obscure words of that same God so hidden and unknowable. They are rays of light in an ocean of darkness. Every ray, every stream of light, come from it. The fall of angels, that of Adam, the wickedness and idolatry of men before and after the deluge; the lives of the patriarchs, who knew and recounted to their children the story of creation; every recent discovery; these are the obscure words of the Holy Scriptures. A handful of men saved from idolatry in the universal ruin of the world up to the coming of the Messiah, wickedness always triumphant, always powerful, that small band of defenders of the faith always persecuted and abused, the treatment of Jesus Christ, the plagues of the apocalypse; can these indeed be the words of God, what he has revealed, what he has ordained? And the effects of these fearful mysteries, moreover, which continue till the end of time, are they the living word teaching us wisdom, strength and goodness? Although it is not evident, alas, we must believe it! All the divine attributes proclaim it through everything that happens in the world. It is all a parable.

What was God saying to us through unbelievers, protestants, the reformation? All intimate as clearly as daylight his eternal truths. Pharaoh and all pagans who have followed him and still do, demonstrate it. But if we are looking with our eyes only, events tell us the contrary. We must blind ourselves and cease to reason before we can grasp these divine mysteries.

You speak, Lord, to mankind in general through all that happens. All revolutions are merely waves of your divine purpose creating upheavals in the reasoning of restless man. You speak to each one individually through what happens to him from one moment to the next. But instead of hearing the voice of God in it all and respecting the dark mystery of his word, he sees in it only historical events, chance, or the machinations of men, and presumes to find fault with everything. In the name of progress, reform and betterment, he takes the liberty of committing excesses, the least of which would be an abomination if it concerned one comma of the Holy Scriptures. 'This is the word of God, sacred and true', we insist, and not understanding, we only venerate it the more. It is right that we should worship and acknowledge the profound wisdom of God. But, dear sisters, what he is telling us, the words he pronounces moment by moment, whose substance is not ink and paper, but what we do and suffer from one moment to the next, do not these deserve our attention? Why do we not reverence God's truth and goodness in all this? Nothing pleases us, we criticize everything. Do we not realize that we are judging by reason and the senses what can only be judged by faith? And that, if we read the word of God in the scriptures through eyes of faith, it must be wrong to read his works with any other eyes.

Breath of the Holy Spirit

Faith is required for everything divine. If we live continually by faith we shall always be in touch with God, speaking to him face to face. In the same way as our thoughts and words are transmitted by air, so are God's conveyed by all we are given to do and suffer. Not only the substance of his word will be manifest, but everything will be sanctified and perfected for us. In heaven this is glory, and on earth faith, with only a difference of degree, not of kind, between them.

We only truly learn when God speaks directly to us. We do not become wise in the knowledge of God by reading or painstaking historical research; that is a vain pursuit which only confuses and inflates our ego. We learn through what happens to us from one moment to the next. It is that knowledge we gain from experience for which Jesus came on earth to teach us. Being God, he already knew everything, but for us it is essential if we wish to speak to the hearts of those whom God sends us.

We can only know through our suffering and our actions what experience has taught us. It is the breath of the Holy Spirit whispering the words of life to the heart, and everything we say to others must come from this source. What we read and what we see only becomes divine knowledge through the fruits, the virtue and the light we gain from it. It is merely the dough, leaven is needed and salt to season it; without them ideas remain vague and we are like visionaries who know every road in the town but cannot find their way home. And so we must listen each moment to God in order to become learned in that divine theology which is founded on practice and experience. Ignore what is told to others, listen to what is told to you only. It will confirm your faith and by its very obscurity will purify, intensify and strengthen it.

Faith, by the light it sheds, becomes God's interpreter. We don't even realize that God is speaking; we hear only the confused language of human beings signifying nothing but misery and death. Faith teaches us that the essence of wisdom is understanding which reveals meaning, so that we see only eloquence and divine perfection in all the pompous nonsense and jargon of human beings. Faith gives the whole earth a celestial aspect; by it the heart is transported, enraptured to commune with heaven. Each moment is a revelation of God.

Everything remarkable about the lives of the saints, their visions, their inner voices, is only a pale reflection of their continuing state of rapture which comes from the practice of their faith. To live is to find it in all that happens moment by moment. When this rapture shines visibly it does not mean that it was not there already, but that it shines in order to manifest all its wonders and to inspire souls in the practice of faith, just as the glory of the transfiguration and the miracles of Jesus Christ were not just to demonstrate his perfection. They were flashes of light from time to time in the dark cloud of humanity, to make it more acceptable.

God's Instruments, Moment by Moment

The miracle of the saints lies in their life of continuing faith in all things. Without it, all the rest of their visions, and the voices they hear, would all fall short of that holiness which consists in the loving faith that makes them rejoice in God and see him in all things. This does not require miracles; they are only for the benefit of those who need such testimonies and signs. Faithful souls do not rely on them. Content in their unknowing, they leave them to be a light for others, and accept for themselves all that is most ordinary: God's order, God's way which tests their faith by concealing not revealing himself. Faith needs no proofs. Those who need them have little faith, but those who live by faith receive proof, not as such, but through God's purpose. In this sense, miracles are not inconsistent with perfect faith, for it happens that in the many saints whom God creates for the salvation of souls, there exist proofs to enlighten the feeblest. Such were and always will be the prophets, the apostles and all the saints through whom God chooses to shine forth his light. They have always existed and always will, but hidden in the Church, too, are countless saints who are made only to shine in heaven, who shed no light in this life and who live and die in complete obscurity.

We must drink from the spring to quench our thirst; sipping only makes us more thirsty. Similarly if we wish to think, write and live like prophets, the apostles and the saints, we must abandon ourselves, like them, to God's purpose for us.

O mystery of love! We imagine that miracles are over, and that all we can do now is to copy your works of old and repeat your ancient words! We do not see that your continuing operation is an everlasting source of fresh ideas, fresh suffering and action, of new prophets, patriarchs, apostles and saints who have no need to follow in each other's footsteps, but live in a continuing abandonment to your secret intentions. We are always hearing 'The first centuries—the age of saints!' What a way to talk! Is not all time a succession of the consequences of that divine action which pervades and fills and transfigures everything? Was there ever in ancient times a way of submitting to it which is not forever acceptable? Did those saints of old have any secret other than to become each moment of their lives God's instruments? And will that divine action cease till the end of time to pour its grace over souls who surrender themselves totally to it?

Yes, O Blessed Love, adorable, everlasting, eternally merciful, ever miraculous! Work of my God, you are my book, my wisdom, my understanding. You are my thought, my words, my deeds, my suffering. It is not by considering what you are doing elsewhere that I shall become what you wish me to. It is by accepting your presence in everything, that ancient and royal way of my fathers. I shall think, be enlightened and talk like them. That is the way in which I shall emulate, quote and follow them all.

It is only because we fail to take full possible advantage of divine action that we turn to so many alternatives. Such diversity cannot give us what we find in that singleness of purpose from which we derive the power to do great things. In Jesus we have a master to whom we do not sufficiently listen. He speaks to each heart the word of life, the only word, but we do not listen. We want to know what he is saying to others, and do not listen to what he is saying to us. We are not sufficiently attuned to that transcendental being imparted to all things by divine action. It deserves our attention, and those who heed it with an open heart and with confidence and courage need fear nothing.

The irresistible force which, from the beginning to the end of time, is changeless, pervades every moment and bestows its unique power on faithful souls who worship, love and rejoice in it alone.

We long for the opportunity to die for God, and to live heroically. To lose all, to die forsaken, to sacrifice ourselves for others; such notions enchant us. But I, heavenly Father, will worship and glorify your purpose, finding in it all the joy of martyrdom, self-sacrifice and duty to my neighbour. This is enough for me, and however your purpose may require me to live or die, I shall remain content. I love it for its own sake, apart from what it achieves, because it pervades, sanctifies and changes everything in me. Everything is glorified, all my moments are filled with your Holy Spirit, and, living and dying, I long only for it.

Yes, dear sisters, though I will always welcome you, I will no longer direct the time or manner of your devotions; it is as though through divine action God's immensity has been revealed to me, and henceforth I shall take no step on my own account, I shall act only within its vast dimension.

Divine action has always been the source from which flows a torrent of grace which spreads over everything. Henceforth I shall no longer seek it within the narrow confines of a book, or the life of a saint, or a sublime idea. These are mere drops in an ocean flowing over all creation, mere atoms lost in the deep. I shall no longer seek God's word in the thoughts of mystics, no longer turn to them, begging my bread, as it were, from door to door, no longer pay them tribute.

Grace Supplies All Needs

For truly, Lord, I long to live worthily of you, the child of a true, infinitely wise, good and powerful father. I wish to live as I believe, and since I know that you work in all things and at all times for my good, I wish to make the best of this immense, certain and always available good fortune. Is there a human creature whose power equals yours? Why should I turn to men who are powerless, ignorant and callous? If I run from fountain to fountain, from stream to stream dying of thirst, there is a hand that brings a flood and water surrounds me everywhere. Everything turns to bread to nourish me, soap to wash me, fire

[71]

to purify me, and a chisel to fashion me in the image of God. Grace supplies all my needs. Should I look for it elsewhere it will always find me and be manifest in all creation.

O heavenly Father, must you be ignored and must you throw yourself and all your loving kindness at everyone's feet, so to speak, while we are searching for you in nooks and crannies where you are not to be found? What folly not to breathe the air, walk with unfaltering step in open country, find water in a flood; not to discover God, not to savour him, not to perceive his bounty in all things!

You are trying to discover the secret of how to belong to God, beloved sisters. But there is none, unless it be to take advantage of every opportunity. Everything leads to union with him; everything brings about perfection excepting sin and what is not our duty. Only take things as they come without interfering. Everything guides, purifies and sustains you, carrying you along, so to speak, under God's banner by whose hand earth, air and water are made divine. His power is vaster and more immense than the elements. It penetrates all the senses if they serve his purpose alone and resist everything not ordained by him. His Holy Spirit pervades every atom in your body, to the very marrow of your bones. Whatever blood flows through your veins, flows by its power. No matter whether you are strong or weak, languid or vigorous, alive or dead, every condition of the human body is the work of grace. All your feeling and thoughts, whatever they may be, come from that invisible source. No human heart or mind can tell how it will affect you; you can only learn through continual experience. Your life flows unceasingly in that unknown deep where all that is necessary is to love and accept the present moment as the best, with perfect trust in God's universal goodness.

Every soul could live in inconceivable and sublime exaltation if all were contented with God's purpose for them. Yes, if we could leave that divine hand to do its work we could all attain the height of perfection. It is offered to us all, we have only to reach out our hand for it. There is not a living soul whose nature is not uniquely sacred, so that all can live, act and speak sublimely. Souls have only to follow each other along the same path and divine action will make each one, though ordinary, unique.

How can I explain to your creatures, O heavenly Father, what I am proposing to them? Is it possible that, possessing such a precious gift and being able to enrich the world, I must watch souls drying up like plants in a desert? Come, simple souls, without a trace of piety, talent or even the most elementary instruction or system, and with no understanding of spiritual matters, who are amazed and overwhelmed by the eloquence of the learned; come, I will show you how to outshine those clever scholars, and will set you so well on your way to perfection that you will always find it at your feet, over your head and all around you. I will unite you to God and you will be led by the hand if you do what I tell you. Come, not only to look at a map of the spiritual country, but to possess it and walk in it without fear of losing your way. Come, not to study the history of God's divine action, but to be its object; not to learn what it has achieved throughout the centuries and still does, but simply to be the subject of its operation. There is no need to bother about what has been told to others; there are words for you alone.

Living Books of the Holy Spirit

This is the universal spirit which pervades every heart, speaking to each one individually. It speaks through Isaiah, Jeremiah, Ezekiel. Without knowing it, all are instruments of that spirit to bring the message ever freshly to the world. And if souls knew how to unite themselves to this purpose, their lives would be a succession of divine scriptures, continuing till the end of time, not written with ink on paper, but on each human heart. This is what the book of life is about. Unlike the holy scriptures, it will not only be a history of the work of the Holy Spirit over the centuries since the world began to the day of judgement. In it will be written down every thought, word, deed and suffering of all souls. And that scripture will then be a complete record of divine action.

And so the sequel to the New Testament is being written now, by action and suffering. Saintly souls are in the succession of the prophets and the Apostles, not by writing canonical books, but by continuing the history of divine purpose with their lives, whose moments are so many syllables and sentences through which it is vividly expressed. The books the Holy Spirit is writing are living, and every soul a volume in which the divine author makes a true revelation of his word, explaining it to every heart, unfolding it in every moment.

Wisdom of the Pure in Heart

In the course of time every truly wise concept is fulfilled by divine action. In the eyes of God everything has its own image which only wisdom can divine. If you were able to conceive all those not meant for you, the knowledge would get you nowhere. Divine action sees the word, the image in which you are to be made, the pattern it proposes and what is most expedient for each one of us. Holy scripture partly contains it, and the inward working of the Holy Spirit according to the word of God achieves the rest. Can we not see that the only secret of conforming to this enduring image is to be pliable under its influence? And that this cannot be done by cleverness, intelligence or subtlety of mind, but by a passive acceptance and yielding, like metal to the mould, canvas to the brush or stone to the chisel? Why do we not see that it is not the study of all those divine and eternal mysteries of God's will, that can make us conform to the image the word has conceived for us—but that it is the impression stamped on us of that mysterious image itself? This impression is not stamped on the soul by ideas, but on the senses by the surrendering of self.

The wisdom of the pure in heart is to be contented with their lot, to keep on their way and never to overreach themselves. They are not curious about how God operates. They accept without question what he ordains for them, waiting only for each moment to reveal God's word, happy and contented in the knowledge that he speaks to the heart. They are not concerned about what he is saying to them or to others. So that from one moment to the next, however little and in whatever way, they are receiving his grace without realizing it. This is how the Lord speaks to his loved ones, fulfilling his purpose in ways they do not understand, being aware only of their earthly suffering and actions. This is how holiness is deeply diffused throughout their whole being. It is not determined by those ideas and turbulent words which, by themselves, only inflate us. Acts of piety are held to be of great importance to the spirit; but they are not necessary and can even be harmful. All that matters is to submit to the suffering and actions ordained by God. And yet we leave that divine substance in order to fill our minds with the historic wonders of this work, instead of adding to them by our faith. Satisfying our curiosity by reading about the wonders of this work only gives us an aversion for those apparently insignificant things by which, if we did not despise them, we could accomplish great ones. How foolish we are to admire and praise divine action in writings which boast about its history, while divine action itself is trying to continue writing, not with ink but in our hearts. We hinder it by continuing impatiently to turn the pages in our curiosity to discover what it is doing in ourselves and others.

Forgive me, divine Love, for speaking only of my shortcomings and not having yet understood what it means to let your will be done, not having allowed myself to be poured into that mould. I have been through all your galleries and admired

all your paintings, but I have not yet surrendered myself sufficiently to be worthy to receive the strokes of your brush. Now I
have at last found you, beloved Master, my Healer, my Lord,
blessed Love! I will be your disciple and learn only from you. I
return like a prodigal son, starving for your bread. I will cease
to traffic in ideas and works of piety, using them only in
obedience to you in this as in all things, and not for my own
satisfaction. I will devote myself exclusively to the duty of the
present moment to love you, to fulfil my obligations and to let
your will be done.

The Only Source of Perfection

When souls discover the divine purpose, they put aside all
pious works, systems, books, ideas, spiritual advisers, in order
to be alone under the sole guidance of God and his purpose
which becomes the only source of perfection for them. They
are in his hands as saints always have been, sure that he alone
knows what is best for them and that, if they were to trust to
human guidance, they would only lose their way in that
uncharted region which God has created in them. And so this
mysterious force directs and leads them by ways it alone knows,
and they drift like air, God manifesting his will from one
moment to the next. Whatever he ordains for them or makes
them do instinctively or by force of circumstances, is all they
know of spirituality. It is their visions, their revelations, the
whole of their wisdom and discretion which never fails them.
Faith assures them that what they are doing is right. They
read, write, talk or think only in order to discover the excellence of divine action as it ordains they should. They submit to
it in this as in all things, accepting its divine sanction, making
use of things seen and things unseen. Always borne up each
moment by faith in that infallible, unchangeable and ever
effective power; rejoicing in and discovering it in all things
both great and small. It fills each moment completely so that

they enjoy everything, not for itself, but trusting in that divine spirit and inner power which they believe underlies it despite appearances to the contrary. And so their lives are not spent in questioning, wishful thinking, contempt or sighs, but in the certainty that what they have is always the best.

Every condition of body and soul, everything that happens both inwardly and outwardly, what each moment reveals, is the fulfilment of divine purpose—it is happiness. Anything more or less is nothing but misery and deprivation, since the only true and just measure of happiness is what God ordains. Therefore whether or not souls are deprived of thought, speech, books, nourishment, companionship, health or even of life itself, does not matter. They adore God's purpose and the equally blessed cross without question, it is enough for things to *be* to win their approval. What does not exist cannot but be useless.

The present moment is like an ambassador announcing the policy of God; the heart declares 'Thy will be done', and souls, travelling at full speed, never stopping, spread the news far and wide. For them everything without exception is an instrument and means of sanctification, providing that the present moment is all that matters. It is no longer a question of supplication or silence, reticence or eloquence, reading or writing, ideas or apathy, neglect or study of spiritual books, affluence or destitution, sickness or health, life or death. All that matters is what the will of God ordains each moment. This is the casting off, the withdrawal from, the renunciation of, the world, not actually but in effect, to be nothing by or for ourselves, to belong totally to God, to please him, making our sole happiness to look on the present moment as though nothing else in the world mattered.

God's Ineffable Will
If everything that happens to souls who have surrendered

themselves to God is all that matters, it must be true that having everything there is nothing to complain of, and if they do complain, they are lacking in faith and living by their reason and their senses, which do not perceive the sufficiency of grace and can never be satisfied. According to the scriptures, to glorify the name of God is to recognize that he is holy, to adore and love him for everything he utters. Everything God does each moment tells us something significant, manifesting his purpose in so many words and sentences. His purpose is but one in itself, incomprehensible, unutterable; but its effects are countless and known by as many names. To glorify the name of God is to know, worship and love that adorable, incomprehensible word which is his very essence. It is also to recognize and adore and worship his ineffable will every moment in all its manifestations, seeing everything as mere glimmers and shadows of that eternally divine purpose, divine in all its works, all its utterance, all its manifestations, and by what ever name. This is how Job called down the blessing on the name of God. The total desolation by which his will was made known was blessed by this holy man in the name of God—not cursed— and, in blessing it, Job affirmed that the most terrible manifestation of God's divine purpose was nevertheless sacred whatever form it might take, just as David blessed it always in whatever circumstances. And so it is by this continual discovery, this manifestation, this revelation of the divine purpose of God in all things, that his kingdom is in us, that his will is done on earth as it is in heaven, that he gives us our daily bread. His purpose includes and contains the substance of that incomparable prayer, dictated by Jesus, which, as ordained by God and the holy Church, we recite aloud several times a day, but which we also repeat every moment from the bottom of our heart as we rejoice in all we do and suffer in obedience to his word. What the lips take many syllables, sentences and time to pronounce, the heart is really saying all the time. This is how faithful souls must glorify God in the depths of their being, though they groan at being powerless to do so in any other way, so like adversity are the means God employs to bestow his grace and favours on them. Herein lies the secret of divine wisdom, to impoverish the senses while enriching the heart. The emptiness of one makes the fullness of the other, and this is so universally true that the more holy the heart, the less the outward eye can detect it.

Celestial Manna

Everything that happens each moment bears the stamp of God's will. How holy is that name! How right to worship it for its own sake! Can we look on him who bears it without infinite reverence? It is celestial manna falling from the sky, pouring down grace; it is the holy kingdom in the soul, it is the bread of angels consumed on earth as it is in heaven. No moment is trivial since each one contains a divine kingdom, and heavenly sustenance.

O heavenly Father! May your kingdom enter my heart to sanctify, nourish, purify and make it triumph over my enemies. Precious moment, how small in the eyes of my head and how great in those of my heart, the means whereby I receive small things from the Father who reigns in heaven! Everything that falls from there is very excellent, everything bears the mark of its maker.

It is just, O Lord, that those who are not satisfied with the divine bounty of the present moment, which pours down on them from the Father of Light, should be punished by being unable to find contentment in anything. If books, the lives of the saints, spiritual intercourse, bring us no peace it means that we are not surrendering ourselves to the duty of the present moment, and that we are stuffing our minds out of mere greed. Such repletion is unacceptable for it leaves no room for God. But if they have been divinely sanctioned we must accept them as the word of God, and take them on trust like everything else, for the sake of obedience; to be put aside as soon as the time for ideas is over, to return to peace and contentment in the present moment.

Divine action often brings to mystical books a meaning their authors never had. For God uses the words and actions of others to reveal truths which they never intended. This is the way God tells us his truths, and souls committed to him must take advantage of it. Every means used by divine action is always more effective and surpasses human virtue in excellence.

Those who have abandoned themselves to God always lead mysterious lives and receive from him exceptional and miraculous gifts by means of the most ordinary, natural and chance experiences in which there appears to be nothing unusual. The simplest sermon, the most banal conversations, the least erudite books become a source of knowledge and wisdom to these souls by virtue of God's purpose. This is why they carefully pick up the crumbs which clever minds tread under foot, for to them everything is precious and a source of enrichment. They exist in a state of total impartiality, neglecting nothing, respecting and making use of everything.

When God exists in all things, our enjoyment of his word is not of this earth, it is a delight in his gifts which are transmitted through many different channels. They do not in themselves sanctify us, but are instruments of the divine action which is able to communicate God's grace to the simple, and often does, in ways which seem contradictory. It can shine its light equally well through opaque clay or the finest dust, and the means it chooses are always unrivalled. The faithful know always that they lack nothing. They never grumble about not having the means to do what they think will advance them, because they are supplied in full by their maker. In his divine will lies the whole blessing of men.

The Bounty of the Present Moment

The mind, with all that goes with it, wishes to take the lead in spiritual matters. It must be reduced to nothing and subdued like a dangerous slave, whose simple heart, if he knew how to make use of it, could serve him to great advantage. It could also cause a great deal of damage if not properly controlled. When souls long for tangible action their heart is informed that God's purpose suffices. When they wish truly to renounce all worldly activity, it is informed that it is a measure they must neither accept nor reject, but must meekly comply with God's will, doing everything yet doing nothing, having nothing yet possessing all. Human activity, being substitute for fulfilment, leaves no room for the true fulfilment of divine purpose. But when divine action fulfils this purpose in earthly terms, it brings a true increase of holiness, innocence, purity and disinterestedness. We honour a prince himself by honouring him together with all his retinue. He would be insulted were we not to, under the pretext of honouring him alone. Applying the same argument to God's order, God was holy in the beginning, is now and ever shall be, there are no moments which are not filled with his infinite holiness so that there are none we should not honour.

If what God himself ordains especially for us does not satisfy us, where else shall we turn? If we do not relish what the Holy Spirit prepares for us, what food would not be tasteless to so depraved a palate? Our souls can only be truly nourished, strengthened, enriched and sanctified by the bounty of the present moment. What more can we ask? Since this is how God ordains that things should be, how can we wish them to be otherwise? Can his wisdom and goodness be wrong? Can we doubt their excellence? And so we must conclude that God's purpose is perfection since it emanates from his will, and nowhere else can we find holiness, however saintly in itself, which so well accomplishes our salvation.

How faithless the world is! How unworthily we think of God, since we incessantly find fault with his purpose, in a way we would not dare to do with the work of the most humble craftsman! And yet we presume to do so, confined by the rules and limitations of our feeble reason, though claims to improve it can be no more than grumbles and murmurings. We are surprised at the way Jews treated Jesus Christ. Ah, divine love! adorable will! Everlasting power! How dare we judge you? Can your divine will be unacceptable or at fault?

When one says 'But I am troubled; something is wrong; how unreasonable that this sickness seizes me while I yet retain my health!' I reply 'No, nothing is wrong. The will of God is all that is needed, everything else is useless.' If you know it, when you say everything is misfortune, disappointment, irrelevance, unreasonableness and vexation, you are blaspheming. Although you don't realize it, it is the will of God being blasphemed by his beloved children who do not know what they are doing.

When you were on earth, O Jesus, the Jews accused you of magic and called you a samaritan. And today, in what veneration we hold your beloved word, you who have lived from generation to generation ever worthy of praise and worship! Has there ever been a single moment since the world began to the present day, or will there ever be till the day of judgement, in which the holy word of God is not revered? That word that fills all time and everything that happens in it, which makes all things holy! What? Can what goes by the name of the will of God harm me? Should I dread and fly from that name? And where should I look to find something preferable if I dread God's purpose for me, since it is the consequence of his divine will?

How should we listen to that inner voice continually speaking to our hearts? If our understanding and our reason cannot hear or grasp the truth and holiness of those words, is it not because they are blind to divine truth? Should we be amazed that reason is baffled by a mystery? God's word is a mystery, and therefore death to our senses and reason; for mysteries by their very nature destroy them. Mystery lives in the heart through faith, everything else denies it. Divine purpose both kills and quickens with one stroke; the closer to death the more it seems to bring life; the darker and more obscure the mystery, the more light it sheds. It is why the pure of heart find nothing more divine than what seems least so. This is the living faith.

10. The Secret of the Spiritual Life

God's Veiled Purpose

All creatures live by the hand of God. The senses can only grasp the work of man, but faith sees the work of divine action in everything. It sees that Jesus Christ lives in all things, extending his influence over the centuries so that the briefest moment and the tiniest atom contain a portion of that hidden life and its mysterious work. Jesus Christ, after his resurrection, surprised the disciples when he appeared before them in disguise, only to vanish as soon as he had declared himself. The same Jesus still lives and works among us, still surprises souls whose faith is not sufficiently pure and strong. There is no moment when God is not manifest in the form of some affliction, obligation or duty. Everything that happens to us, in us, and through us, embraces and conceals God's divine but veiled purpose, so that we are always being taken by surprise and never recognize it until it has been accomplished. If we could pierce that veil and if we were vigilant and attentive, God would unceasingly reveal himself to us and we would rejoice in his works and in all that happens to us. We would say to everything: 'It is the Lord!' And we would discover that every circumstance is a gift from God; that human beings, frail creatures though they are, will never lack anything; and that God's unceasing concern is to give them what is best for them. If we had faith, we would be grateful to all creatures, we would bless them and inwardly thank them for contributing, under God's hand, so favourably to our perfection.

Faith is the mother of tenderness, trust and joy. It has only love and compassion for its enemies who benefit so greatly at its expense. The harder the work of mortal man the better God's work makes it for the soul. Only the material he is working with hinders it; but the hand of that celestial turner is merciless in stripping the soul of everything harmful. God's will has only tenderness, mercy and enrichment for those who surrender themselves to it. It can never be too much trusted or too closely obeyed. Faith never doubts that, provided we do not interfere, God's purpose for us is always what will contribute most to our good. The more the senses distrust, rebel, despair, the more faith tells them: 'It is God's will, all is well.' There is nothing that faith cannot overcome; it triumphs over everything and, however dark the clouds may be, it breaks through to truth, holds fast to it and never lets it go.

The Grace of Simplicity

I have more to fear from my own actions and my friends' than those of my enemies. There is no prudence to equal that of non-resistance to one's enemies, of opposing them simply by giving in. It is like sailing before the wind. One has only to sit still and let the galley slaves bring the vessel into port with all hands aboard. There is nothing more certain to resist the wiles of the flesh than simplicity; it effectively evades every trick without recognizing them or even being conscious of doing so. Divine action can make simple souls take exactly the right steps to surprise those who wish to surprise them, and even to profit by their attempts to do so. They are buoyed up by humiliation, every vexation becomes a blessing, and, by leaving their adversaries alone, they derive such a lasting and satisfactory benefit that all they need to think about is being on God's side and doing work inspired by his will, whose instruments their enemies are. Souls have but to look serenely on at what God is doing and humbly follow it, successfully led by the heavenly insight of the Holy Spirit, which invariably influences circumstances and directs them so aptly without their knowing that whatever opposes them is always destroyed.

The unique and infallible power of divine action always influences the simple in the right way, inwardly directing them to react wisely to everything. They welcome all that comes their way, everything that happens to them, everything they experience excepting sin. Sometimes this happens consciously; but sometimes simple souls are moved by mysterious impulses, unconsciously to say, do or ignore things, often for quite natural reasons, in which they see no mystery; things which seem like pure chance, necessity or convenience and seem even to have no significance either to themselves or to others. And yet divine action, in the form of the intelligence, wisdom and advice of their friends, uses them all for the benefit of these souls, ingeniously foiling the plans of those who scheme to harm them. To deal with the pure of heart is to deal with God.

The Magi Have Only to Follow Their Star

How can we resist the Almighty, whose ways are inscrutable? God champions their cause and they have no need to beware of intrigues, or to meet suspicion with suspicion by watching every move against them. Their beloved relieves his children of all this anxiety. And, untroubled and safe, they leave all to him. Divine action delivers and exempts souls from all that sordid mistrust so necessary in human affairs. It may be all right for a Herod or the Pharisees, but the Magi have only to follow their star, and the infant Jesus only to lie in his mother's arms, and their enemies will do them more good than harm.

The more the enemy tries to mislead and thwart souls, the more bold and unperturbed they will be. They will not stoop to sue with him or repel his attack or placate his envy and suspicion. They need persecution. This was how Jesus Christ lived in Judea, and still lives in the same way in the pure of heart. He is noble, loving, free, serene, and fearless, depending on no man, seeing all creatures under God's hand eager to serve him, some by their evil passions, others by their saintly actions, these by their wilfulness, those by their obedience and submission. Divine action arranges it all miraculously, not too much or too little but just the amount of good and evil needed. God provides each moment with its appropriate purpose, and the pure of heart, uplifted by faith, find everything good and wish for neither more nor less than what they have. They continually bless that divine hand which pours its living water over them; they treat their friends and enemies alike with the same gentleness, since it was Jesus' way to treat everyone as divine. They are free agents and yet, at the same time, dependent on each other. What is ordained by divine action is essential, and souls must accept it accordingly and respond to it in humble obedience, being all things to all men, as St Paul told us and Jesus Christ practised even more perfectly. Only grace can impart this spiritual quality which distinguishes and is so marvellously adapted to each one of us. This cannot be learnt through books. It is the true voice of prophecy, an inner revelation, the doctrine of the Holy Spirit. In order to understand it, it is necessary to be in a state of total self-surrender, completely detached from every purpose and every interest, however holy, to have no other interest in the world than passively to submit to divine action in order to devote oneself to the duty of one's state, allowing the Holy Spirit to act in us regardless of what it is doing, happy, even, to remain in ignorance. What happens in this world is often solely for the benefit of souls committed to the will of God.

God's Order and Satan's Disorder

On the face of it the world appears to be of gold, bronze, iron and clay. But this evil mystery is only the confused amalgam of all the seen and unseen actions of the children of darkness; a monster who has come up from hell to wage war on the inner and spiritual man from the beginning of time, and all that has happened since is but a continuation of that war. Monsters succeed one another, hell devours and disgorges them, incessantly belching out fresh fumes. The battle begun in heaven between Lucifer and Saint Michael continues. The heart of that proud and envious angel has become a fathomless pit of every kind of evil. He stirred up angel against angel in heaven, and his sole concern since the world began has been to create ever new villains among men to replace those he swallows up. Lucifer rules those who gladly submit to him. This mystery of evil is nothing but a rejection of God's order; it is the order, or rather the disorder, of the devil; and the mystery of this disorder is, that beneath an alluring exterior it conceals unmitigated and unfathomable evil. All those blasphemers, since the time of Cain to those who devastate the world today, have appeared as splendid and powerful princes making a great stir in the world. But this impression is misleading and a mystery; they are beasts who have come up from hell one after the other to overthrow God's order. But that order, which is yet another mystery, has always opposed them with truly great and powerful men, who have delivered a mortal blow to those monsters, and as hell disgorges new ones, heaven also gives birth to heroes to fight them. Ancient history, sacred and profane, is only the history of that war in which God's order has always been triumphant, together with those of his side who have gained eternal happiness. Wrong has never been able to protect deserters, it has only repaid them by death—eternal death.

We imagine ourselves to be invincible when we are bent upon evil. O Lord! What a way to try to resist you! With hell and the world against them, those who are on the side of God's order need have no fear. That monstrous image, that head of gold, silver, bronze and iron, is nothing but a phantom of glittering dust which a pebble disperses like chaff blown about by the wind.

How admirably the Holy Spirit unfolds the drama of every age. So many revolutions, which overtake and cast down men who rise so splendidly and soar like meteors above the heads of their fellows. So many astounding events; all a Nebuchadnezzar's dream forgotten on waking, however terrifying their impressions may have been.

All these monsters only come into the world to try the courage of the children of God. Who, having learnt their lesson, he allows the satisfaction of killing their enemy, and then heaven carries off the victor and hell swallows up the vanquished; and when another monster appears, God calls fresh athletes into the field of battle. Our life is a continual drama which rejoices heaven, exercises saints, and brings confusion in hell; in this way everything which resists God's order only serves to make it more revered. Every enemy of his order is a victim of God's justice, and divine action builds a heavenly Jerusalem on the foundations of Babylon which are but broken stones and rubble.

What use is the most sublime enlightenment and divine revelation if we do not love the will of God? Lucifer could not abide it; the power of his divine purpose, which God disclosed to him by revealing the mystery of the incarnation, only made him envious. But the pure of heart, by the light of faith alone, never cease to worship, praise and adore God's order; to find it not only in holy things but also in the most chaotic disorder and confusion. One grain of perfect faith enlightens the pure of heart more than Lucifer ever was by all his own pretensions to wisdom.

The Weapon of Gentle Yielding

The understanding of souls who are faithful to their duties, quietly obeying the inmost movement of grace, meek and humble in all things, is worth more than the most penetrating insight into mystery. If only we were able to perceive God's action in all the egotism and arrogance of humans we would have nothing but respect for them. Their chaos can never replace order whatever they do, and this uniting of God's action with his creatures through humility and meekness must never be abandoned; we must not look which way others are going but follow confidently our own, and thus by gentle yielding we break through forests and overturn mountains. For what creature can resist the force of a faithful, meek and humble soul? If we wish unfailingly to conquer our adversaries, we need only oppose them with these weapons. Jesus Christ has placed them in our hands for our defence and we have nothing to fear if we know how to use them. We must be courageous, not cowardly, since the power of divine action consists only in courage. God performs sublime wonders, and no power fighting him can conquer one which is united to his divine action through gentleness and humility.

What is Lucifer? A clever spirit, the most enlightened of all, but one discontented with God and his order. The mystery of evil is nothing but the outcome of this discontent which manifests itself in every possible way. Lucifer tries with all his might to leave nothing as God has ordained and created it; wherever he goes God's disfigured work can be seen.

The more enlightened, intelligent and capable a person is, the more he is to be feared if he does not have that fundamental goodness which consists in being contented with God and his will. A steadfast heart unites us to divine action. Without it all is purely human nature and usually pure contradiction to God's order, which has not, to tell the truth, any other instruments than the meek. He is always resisted by the proud, who,

however, never cease to serve him as slaves in the accomplishment of his designs. When I see people whose all is God and
submission to his order, however devoid they may be of everything else, I say: 'These are people who have a great gift for
serving God.' They are like the holy Virgin and Saint Joseph.
Everything else I suspect, fearing to discover Lucifer's hand in
it. On my guard, I resolve in my heart to fight him, and then all
that tangible glitter appears to me like fragile glass.

Let There Be Light

God's order is the whole wisdom of the pure of heart. They
reverence it in those acts of defiance which the proud do to dis-
parage it. The proud despise the meek in whose eyes they are
nothing, seeing only God in all they do. The proud often
imagine that humility is a sign that the meek fear them, when
it is only a sign of their love and fear of God and his will which
the meek see in the proud. No, poor fools, the meek are not
afraid of you, they pity you. It is to God they are speaking when
you imagine they are addressing you. It is with him they are
dealing and they look upon you as one of his slaves, or rather as
a fog disguising him. And so the more arrogant your tone, the
more humble theirs. Your cunning and profligacy to them are
merely the grace of providence. Moreover, pride is an enigma
which the meek enlightened by faith can explain very easily.
This discovery of divine action in everything that happens,
each moment, is the most subtle wisdom possible regarding
the ways of God in this life. It is a continual revelation, an ever
renewed communion with him. It is joy in the beloved, not in
secrecy or stealth behind closed doors or in drunken stupor,
but openly in public, without fear of anyone or anything. It is a
fount of peace, joy and love; of contentment in God, seen,
known, experienced, and perfecting all that happens every
moment. It is everlasting paradise which is at present only a
shapeless mass lost in clouds; but the Spirit of God, who

secretly arranges everything in this life with that continuing and abounding activity, will say on the day of death: 'Let there be light! *Fiat Lux!*' We will then see the treasures faith holds in that ocean of peace and contentment in God, which is found in all that is to be done and suffered.

When God manifests himself in this way nothing seems extraordinary, because everything is made to seem remarkable. It is the way itself that is amazing, and consequently there is no need to adorn it with any other miracles which don't belong to it. It is a miraculous, everlasting revelation and rejoicing; though in itself there is nothing noticeably miraculous about it. Like the holy Virgin, it sheds over all ordinary things a shining glory.

11. The Dark Night of Faith

The Experience of Passive Saintliness

There is a kind of saintliness when divine communication is precise and clear as daylight. But there is also a passive saintliness communicated by God through faith from the impenetrable darkness which surrounds his throne, in terms that are confused and obscure. Those who find this way are often afraid, like the prophet, to follow it and afraid of running into danger when walking through that darkness. Have no fear, faithful souls! That is where your path lies, the way along which God is guiding you. There is nothing safer or more sure than the dark night of faith. Follow any way when faith is so obscure and darkness obliterates everything and the path can no longer be discerned, for a path cannot be lost which does not exist. But the soul cries out: 'Every moment I seem to be falling down a precipice. I know I am surrendering myself to God, that I can achieve nothing unless I cease to act on the strength of my own virtue. But I hear virtue calling and the more that voice pleases and attracts me the more I am drawn away to that mysterious power, and I yield to its influence even though I love virtue. I cannot see that it is guiding me in the right direction, but I cannot prevent myself from believing that it is.'

The senses run towards the light, but the heart seeks only darkness. All people, every bright spirit, charm the senses; but the heart cares only to converse in a language it does not understand. It is inspired solely by the gift of faith which makes it prefer the source, the truth, the way where the spirit has neither aim nor ideas, where it trembles and falters. Why, I cannot tell, but in my heart, which goes where it is driven, I am reassured, convinced that this influence is good, not by any evidence, but by the knowledge which comes from faith. For it is impossible that God should guide souls without assuring them of the sacredness of his way, which is the more holy the less it seems so. And however they may strive to find something better, this conviction triumphs over all fantasies, fears, endeavours and ideas of the senses. The pure of heart can feel without touching their Lord; if they reach out for him he vanishes. They feel his holiness surrounding them and prefer to submit themselves to his guidance, which leads them aimlessly without order, than to reassure themselves by choosing the well-defined path of virtue.

Come then, since virtue comes from our own ingenuity and effort, let us be resigned to our frailty and dependence on God, who would never reduce us to being unable to walk on our own feet if he had not the mercy to carry us in his arms. What need have we of light, O Lord, to see, feel, have confidence, inspiration or judgement, since we are in your hands? The more pitfalls there are, the more darkness, danger, mortification, dryness, fear, privation, trouble, anguish, despair, persecution, suffering and desolation there is on our way, the more our faith and trust will be strengthened. It will be enough to look to you for reassurance when we are in the utmost peril. We will forget the way and all its twists and turns, we will forget ourselves, and totally surrender ourselves to the wisdom, the mercy and the power of our guide. We will remember only to love you, avoid all sin, both grievous and slight, and fulfil our duty. That is the only responsibility, dear Lord, you leave to your beloved children. You yourself take charge of all the rest. The more terrible that rest is, the more your children will discover and rely on your presence, their only conceren to lose themselves in love, fulfilling their little tasks, like children playing in their mother's lap, as though there was nothing else in the world except their mother and their games. We must look beyond the shadows; night is not the time for action but repose. The light of reason only intensifies the darkness of faith; and the rays that can pierce it must come from on high.

Verses in the Hymns of Night

When God speaks directly to us through life, he no longer appears as the way and the truth. If we seek him in darkness he is behind us, holding our hand, urging us on. But if we seek him face to face, he eludes us. In divine action there are secret and unforeseeable resources; unknown and marvellous ways of dealing with the cares, difficulties, troubles, failures, reverses and anxieties of those who have lost all confidence in themselves. The more confused their situation, the better the charm works and the heart says, 'All will be well!' All is in God's hands, there is nothing to fear. Fear itself, suspense, desolation, are verses in the hymns of night. We rejoice in not omitting a single syllable, for we know they all end in 'Glory be to God!' Thus we find our way by losing it. The clouds themselves guide us, doubts assure us. The more troubled Isaac was about finding a sacrifice, the more Abraham relied on God for everything.

Those who walk in light sing hymns of light; those who walk in darkness sing hymns of darkness. All must sing the part and the tune allotted to them by God, to the end. Nothing must be added to what he has filled; every drop of gall of this divine bitterness must be drained to the dregs to the point of intoxication. Jeremiah and Ezekiel, whose only words were tears and sighs, could never find consolation except in continual lamentations. He who would have stopped the flow of their tears would have removed the most beautiful parts of the scriptures. Pessimists are the only optimists, and the two have the same origin.

When God astonishes souls they tremble, if he threatens them they are terrified. His divine work must be allowed to unfold, it encompasses both evil and its cure.

Weep, dear sisters, tremble in agitation and anguish, make no effort to try to overcome this divine dread, these spiritual groans. Receive in the centre of your being rivulets from that ocean which Jesus carried in his sacred soul. Continue to shed such tears as grace brings to your eyes and imperceptibly dries up. Clouds will vanish, the sun will shine again, spring bring you flowers and the results of your surrender will be to discover the wonderful variety and extent of divine action. Indeed, it is in vain that men are troubled. Everything happens to them as in a dream, one shadow follows and destroys the other, fantasies succeed one another in those who sleep—some torment, others console. The soul is the victim of these fantasies which devour each other; the awakening reveals that they are nothing to be alarmed about; all illusions are dissipated and both the terrors and the joys of the night are forgotten.

How can I explain, Lord, why you keep your children asleep on your bosom through the night of faith and wish to subject them to an infinite variety of experiences which are really holy and mystical reveries? It is because in that darkness and sleep which envelope them, real and painful doubts, anguish and worries assail them which, on the day of glory, you will dispel and turn into true rejoicing.

It is on the point of that awakening and after that these saintly souls, entirely restored to themselves and in full control of their faculties, will never cease to marvel at the skill, ingenuity, shrewdness and loving guile of their Lord. So incomprehensible are his ways that it is impossible to find an answer to his riddles, discover his disguise or find comfort if he wishes to spread alarm and despondency on that awakening. The

Jeremiahs, the Davids, realized that what was a cause for rejoicing to God and his angels, to them was a source of inconsolable despair.

Do not allow the world's clamour to wake these souls; leave them to groan and tremble, pursue and search. It is true that their Lord is evading them, is disguising himself, and that their night of doubt and sorrow is illusory. But let them sleep, let the Lord speak to his cherished ones and show them what he alone knows how to convey and express. Leave him to reveal the rest of that dream. He will waken them when it is time. Did not Joseph, in the Old Testament, make his brothers suffer alarm and misfortune before disclosing to them the greatest cause for rejoicing they had ever known?

The Dark Night of Perfect Faith

Ignorant and naïve quietists, who expect to discover serenity and indifference which never existed in Jesus or Mary, nor in the Davids, the prophets or the Apostles, how little you understand the might of divine action, or the power, variety and range of the dark night of perfect faith! How little you know of the soul's sleep there! How exposed the falseness of your doctrines in the wonderful scenes described in the Song of Songs by the Holy Spirit. All refute your propositions. The state of pure faith is the state of pure suffering. All is dark, all is pain; it is a darkness which covers everything. It is true that souls are resigned and content with God's mercy, but they feel the pain none the less. It is a purgatory in which all feeling and perception are but suffering, the greatest of which is to discover in themselves only resignation and so strong an interest in their own well-being, that God's is a matter of indifference which does not touch them. How great a difference there is between acting on principle, precedent or doctrine, and acting on divine inspiration!

We are driven blindly along a path we have never seen or

heard of, unable to venture along any other. Divine action never follows the same course, it always traces out fresh paths. Those whom it leads never know where they are going; they will not find the way through books or by their own searching. Divine action for ever opens the way which they are compelled to take.

When one is led by a guide who takes one through unknown country by night, across ground without any clearly defined paths, going wherever he fancies without asking advice or disclosing his intentions, what is there but to surrender to him? What is the use of looking to see where one is, asking passers by, or consulting the map and other travellers? All this would defeat the intention and whim, so to speak, of our guide, who demands complete confidence and wishes to arouse anxiety and mistrust in us in order that we should totally depend on him. If we were certain that he was guiding us in the right direction, this would be neither faith nor surrender. Divine action is essentially good and needs no direction or improving. It began with the creation of the world and from that moment has shown ever fresh proof that its power is unlimited and invention inexhaustible. It did that yesterday, this today, being the same action working each moment in new ways, everlastingly unfolding and deploying itself. It fashioned Abels, Noahs, Abrahams, all on different patterns. Isaac was original, Jacob was not his duplicate, nor was Joseph his copy. Moses had no equal among his fathers; David and the prophets were entirely different to the patriarchs, Saint John surpasses them all. Jesus Christ was the first born, without example or doctrine, always freshly inspired, his sacred soul obedient to every breath of the Holy Spirit. The Apostles lived more by the impact of his spirit than by the imitation of his deeds. He never needed to look to the past for a precedent, he was moved by grace according to the pattern of eternal truths contained in the infinite wisdom of the Holy Trinity; and the orders he received moment by moment he outwardly obeyed. The Gospel shows us how these truths affected his life, and the same Jesus lives among us still, working ever freshly in saintly souls.

If you wish to live according to the gospels, surrender yourselves totally to the work of God. Jesus Christ is the source, he was yesterday and still is today in order to continue his life not to begin it again. What he has done is done, what is to be done is being done always. All of us partake of this divine life; although Jesus Christ is different in each one, he himself remains the same. The life of each individual is the life of Jesus, a new testament. The face of the Lord is like a border of sweetly smelling flowers. Divine action is the gardener who arranges the plants so expertly that the border is unlike any other. Among all the flowers there is not one alike, except in their common surrender to the hand of the gardener, leaving him complete mastery over them, to do what he likes, content for their part to do what is their nature and state to do. Let God's will be done; that is the whole of scripture, the universal law.

This, then, is the easy, straightforward, true work of all divine operations. It is the only secret of surrender, an open secret, an art without artistry. It is the straight path which God requires everyone to follow, explains very clearly and makes very simple. What is obscure about perfect faith does not lie in what we must do, but in what God reserves for himself. There is nothing clearer or easier to understand than the first. The only mystery lies in what God himself accomplishes. Take, for example, what happens in the Eucharist! What is necessary to change the body of Jesus Christ is so clear and easy that everyone, however simple, is able to do it if he has a mind to. And yet it remains the mystery of mysteries in which all is so secret, unseen and incomprehensible that the more spiritual and enlightened we are, the more faith we need to believe. The path of perfect faith is somewhat similar. It leads to the discovery of God in each moment, and that is the most exalted, the most spiritual of all blessings. It is an inexhaustible fount of thought, words and writing; an assembly and source of all miracles. But what is needed to produce so prodigious a result? Let God's will be done; obey him in everything, each one according to his capacity. Nothing is easier in the spiritual life, nothing more available to all. Here, then, is that miracle, that unknown way to follow which we need to have great faith, since reason is always suspicious, always finding fault. To be obliged to believe what we cannot see? Nothing we have ever read tells us this! This is something new! 'The prophets were saints, that Jesus was a spellbinder', said the Jews. Ah, what little faith have those who take their view!

Jesus Lived and Lives Still

Jesus lives and works among us, throughout our lives, from the beginning of time to the end, which is but one day. He has lived and lives still. The life he began continues in his saints for ever. O life of Jesus, which includes and outlives all generations! Life eternally renewed! When the world cannot contain everything that could be written about Jesus, about what he did and said, about his own life; when the gospels have only sketched in a few details; when the first hour is so unknown and yet so fateful—what an infinite number of gospels would be required to record the history of every moment of that mystical life whose miracles continually multiply! They will continue till the end of time, since, in fact, time is but the history of divine action! The Holy Spirit has picked out in clear and unmistakable characters a few moments of that vast duration of time, preserved in the scriptures a few drops of that ocean, revealed the secret and mysterious way in which Jesus appeared on earth. We can trace through the arteries and veins the confused mixture of the children of men, the origin, race, genealogy of that first born. The whole of the Old Testament is but a single narrow path through the mysterious labyrinth of highways; the only one that leads to Jesus. The rest remains hidden in the wisdom of the Holy Spirit, which reveals in all that ocean of divine action only a tiny rivulet which, having made its way to Jesus, lost itself in the apostles and was destroyed in the Apocalypse. So the rest of the story, which consists of the whole mystical life of Jesus in the souls of saints, remains a matter of our faith. Everything that has been written about it makes this only too evident. We are in an age of faith, the Holy Spirit no longer writes gospels, except in our hearts; saintly souls are the pages, suffering and action the ink. The Holy Spirit is writing a living gospel with the pen of action, which we will only be able to read on the day of glory when, fresh from the presses of life, it will be published.

O what a beautiful story! What a beautiful book the Holy Spirit is now writing! It is in the press, not a day passes when the type is not being set, the ink not applied, the pages not being printed. But we remain in the night of faith, the paper is darker than the ink; we cannot make out the print, it is in the language of another world which we cannot understand; it is a gospel we will only be able to read in heaven. If we could look at life and see all creatures, not themselves, but their meaning; if we could moreover see the living God in all things, see how divine action motivates, mingles, urges and drives them in opposite directions, we would recognize that everything has its reasons, its place, importance and relevance in this divine work. But how can a book be read, the letters of which are undecipherable, countless, upside down and smudged with ink? If we cannot understand how a jumble of twenty-six letters are sufficient to compose an infinite number of different volumes, each admirable in their way, who can describe what God does in the universe? Who could read and understand so vast a book, in which there is not one letter which does not have its special meaning and which contains, in its small dimension, the most profound mysteries? — mysteries neither seen nor felt, but which are the substance of faith. And faith can judge their truth and their goodness only by their origin. In themselves they are so obscure that, in the light of reason alone, they remain a closed book.

The Book of Life

Teach me, Holy Spirit, to read this book of life! I will be your disciple, and, like an innocent child, believe what I cannot see. It is enough for me that my Lord is speaking. He says this, he declares that, he arranges words in this way. That is enough, I believe everything he has spoken. It is the truth; why I do not know. All he says, all he sees is the truth. He ordains that such letters shall make a word, certain others another. Whether there are three or six, exactly that number are needed. Less would make no sense. He alone knows what letters will spell his thoughts. Everything has a significance, an exact meaning. This line must end here, not a comma is missing, nor a stop unnecessary. Now I believe, but when the day of glory reveals all its mysteries to me, I will see that what I now only dimly understand and which seems to me so perplexing, confused, inconsequential and senseless, will enchant and unceasingly charm me by the beauty, order, wisdom and incomprehensible wonders I shall discover.

All that we see is only vanity and lies. The truth is in God. What a vast difference there is between God's conception and our fantasies! How is it that, being continually reminded that everything that happens in the world is but a shadow, an image, the mystery of faith, we persist in relying only on our human faculties, and continue to interpret the merely temporal aspect of the unanswerable enigma of our existence? Like fools we continually fall into the trap instead of lifting our eyes and going back to the beginning, the source, the origin of things, where everything has another name, another shape; where everything is transcendental, divine, holy; where everything is part of the bounty of Jesus Christ, where everything is a foundation stone of a heavenly Jerusalem, that glorious city where all are invited and all can enter. We live as we see and feel, and make no use of the light of faith which would guide us so safely through all the labyrinths, darkness and fantasies among which we wander foolishly for lack of faith which sees God, and only God, and lives always in him, leaving behind and going beyond appearances.

Faith Is the Light of Time

Faith is the light of time, it alone recognizes truth without seeing it, touches what it cannot feel, looks upon this world as though it did not exist, sees what is not apparent. It is the key to celestial treasures, the key to the unfathomable mystery and knowledge of God. Faith conquers all the fantasy of falsehood; through faith God reveals and manifests himself, deifying all things. Faith removes the veil and uncovers eternal truth. When souls are given the understanding of faith, God speaks to them through all creation, and the universe becomes for them a living testimony which the finger of God continually traces before their eyes, the record of every passing moment, a sacred scripture. The sacred books which the Holy Spirit has dictated are only the beginning of divine guidance for us. Everything that happens is a continuation of the scriptures, expounding for us what has not been written. Faith explains the one through the other. It is an abstraction presenting the vast extent of divine action summarized in the scriptures, in which souls can discover the key to all its mysteries.